Sutherland

Sutherland

A Historical Guide

Robert Gourlay

Birlinn

First published in Great Britain, 1996,
by Birlinn Ltd,
14 High Street,
Edinburgh EH1 1TE

© Robert Gourlay, 1996

The moral right of the author has been asserted.

British Library Cataloguing-in-Publication Data
A Catalogue record for this book is available from the British Library.

ISBN 1 874744 44 0

Typeset in Plantin Light

Printed and bound by Werner Söderström OY, Finland

DEDICATION

For some sixteen years I worked in Highland Region, and came to know it well, in particular the County of Sutherland. I have now moved on, but I would like to take the opportunity provided by this book to thank the many people of Sutherland and beyond who have helped and assisted me in my work by providing a bed for the night, tramping the hills with me, or drawing my attention to new sites or new features of old ones. They are many, and I have no space to thank them all, but in particular I would like to dedicate this volume on Sutherland to Eliot and Pat Rudie of Bettyhill with many, many thanks.

CONTENTS

PREFACE

This book is one of a series describing the archaeological and historical treasures of areas throughout Scotland. In this case, because of the huge area to be covered, and the immense richness of the prehistoric remains, it covers only the period before the emergence of the historical Picts – they, the Vikings, and the subsequent history of Sutherland as seen from its visible remains – must wait for the next volume.

Sutherland is the most north-westerly of the mainland counties of Scotland, stretching from Cape Wrath to Drum Hollistan along the north coast; southwards to Lochinver and Ledmore on the west; and as far as Ardgay in the south-east. It isolates the quite different county of Caithness completely, ringing its flat plateau with a curve of high ground.

Geographically, it would have been, since earliest times, subject to very varied influences. The west coast looks seawards to the Hebrides – land communication being almost non-existent until the military roads of the 18th century were built. From the north coast, Orkney would have been as accessible as anywhere, and influences may have come from the north in the prehistoric period, as they clearly did from the heyday of the Vikings almost up to the present day. By contrast, the east coast looks across the Moray Firth to the rest of Scotland, and over the North Sea towards Europe. The easier landscape is always likely to have made communication with the rest of the mainland much simpler than elsewhere.

In order to find the many sites described in this volume, it is suggested that anyone wishing to visit acquires the necessary Ordnance Survey Landranger maps at a scale of 1:50,000. About seven will be needed (sheets 9, 10, 15, 16, 17, 20 and 21). While the 1:25,000 Pathfinder maps would be better, there are perhaps too many of these for all but the most determined.

Finally, a warning. With the exception of the Archaeological Trail at Ord Hill, Lairg and the brochs at Carn Liath, Golspie and Dun Dornagil, Strath More, *none of these sites have open public access.* The visitor *must*, therefore, seek permission or advice from the nearest house, farm or estate office before visiting. This is in most cases unlikely to be a problem, but there is a need to ensure that activities, where your presence would be disruptive or dangerous – such as at lambing times or during deer-stalking – do not conflict with the local people.

Remember to observe the Country Code at all times. Do not leave litter; leaves gates as you find them; keep dogs (if they are allowed on the land) under proper control, and never take them where there are animals about. Take great care where you park on the mainly single-track roads, so that you cause no hazard to other road-users and do not block access roads or tracks. In particular, do not park in passing places. Also, it is important to let other traffic overtake without delay. These roads are lifelines for remote communities, and you could be holding up emergency services.

Please also respect the monuments and do not move stones or interfere with them in any way, and never use a metal detector on any archaeological site. If you find anything new or of interest, or if monuments have been recently damaged, please contact the Highland Archaeology Service on 01463–711176 and report what you have seen.

ACKNOWLEDGEMENTS

Many people have assisted, directly or indirectly, with the gathering of material for this volume. In particular, thanks are due to many colleagues in the Royal Commission on the Ancient and Historical Monuments of Scotland and in Historic Scotland, especially Piers Dixon and Mike Brooks; Dr Joanna Close-Brooks; staff of Forestry Enterprise, Dornoch, especially Ian Forshaw and Donald MacNeil; and also to Magdalena Donner for help and patience during writing and editing.

FIGURES

MAPS

PLATES

INTRODUCTION

Sutherland is a county of strong contrasts. While much of it is hilly, indeed mountainous in parts, the contrast between the more barren and hospitable north and west, and the greener and more fertile south and east, can be dramatic. The principle reason is the geology of the area, and while there is not space in this volume to go into this in any detail, the traveller will be aware of it wherever he or she goes.

This disparity is reflected in the distribution of archaeological sites, and to some extent, the type of sites that are most prevalent. This should come across very strongly as you read on, and even more forcibly as you travel through the area. Although there are exceptions to the rule – for instance the rich limestone landscape around Durness – the division between north/west and east/south generally holds true. A brief description of the two areas should help understand the landscape, and an understanding of the landscape will assist with understanding the archaeology.

The North and West

Comprising the parishes of Assynt, Eddrachilles, Durness, Tongue and the huge parish of Farr (see Map 1), this area is made up of a hugely long coast with relatively short valleys which flow into the Minch or the Atlantic Ocean. The valley of the rivers Naver and Halladale are exceptional in that they are much longer than the rest and, especially in the case of Strathnaver, rather more fertile. The Durness limestone is another green oasis in a land normally drawn in the colours of rock, water and heather moor.

The area encompasses some wild scenic beauty – stunning sandy beaches between towering cliffs; deep sea lochs penetrating far inland such as Loch Laxford, Loch Inchard, Loch Eriboll, and the softer inlets of the Kyles of Durness and Tongue; hills with famous names and dramatic profiles like Foinaven, Arkle, Ben Stack, Ben Hope and the incomparable Ben Loyal, together with higher but less dramatic mountains like Ben More Assynt and Ben Klibreck – both Munros (over 3000 feet high).

The terrain is dominated by its geology. In the north-west it shows as the 'Cnoc and Lochan' landscape of low, bare, rounded hills interspersed with a myriad small lochs. Around Durness it is the softer, greener flush of grass sweetened by the Durness limestone. In the north are the harsher hills of the Moine rocks. Everywhere are the black peat lands which supply the life-supporting warmth to communities almost devoid of timber resources. A harsh, but beautiful land on the very edge of Europe.

In this part of Sutherland the visitor has to search harder for the remnants of human history than in the softer east and south of Sutherland, but they are here, in pockets of ground fertilised with great effort with shell sand from the beaches, or sometimes in isolated patches where they are least expected.

The South and East

By contrast, the further south and east one goes, the softer and more fertile the landscape becomes. The Dornoch area in particular is green and fertile, although even here, glacial outwash – in the form of drumlins and esker ridges – can be poor in quality and consequently support less evidence of former use.

The coastal strip from Loch Fleet to Helmsdale is narrow, but supports by far the largest communities in modern Sutherland, and has probably always done so. The valleys are broader and richer, and the great wealth of archaeological remains of all periods along the valley sides of rivers like the Shin, Fleet, Brora and Helmsdale, attest to their more favoured geology and climate. Only on the flatter areas along the coast, where modern farming and mechanisation have swept away much of the past, do the number of sites thin out.

Let us now take a trip through time and look at the rich legacy of the past in Sutherland in roughly chronological order.

THE PALAEOLITHIC PERIOD

Before the Last Ice Age

Any remains of pre-glacial human culture in Sutherland should have been entirely wiped out by the inexorable, destructive power of the last Ice Age, except where – by an immeasurably remote chance – some isolated spot escaped its overwhelming force.

Deep in the mountain side, above the tiny hamlet of Inchnadamph (for location see Map 1), lie a number of deep caves in the limestone rock which outcrops in the area, and here, safe even from the grinding of the glaciers, elements of that remote period were preserved. Bones of pre-glacial animals were discovered within what are now known as the 'Bone Caves' but whether or not there is any evidence of *human* activity remains both mysterious and controversial. As I have grave doubts about this myself, I have simply provided a few references in the bibliography for those really interested in following this up. Nevertheless, perhaps in a similar cave elsewhere, fragmentary evidence of this remote period of Scotland's human past may yet be found!

THE MESOLITHIC PERIOD

About 7000 BC to 3000 BC

As the last Ice Age drew to a close, the huge covering of ice which blanketed Scotland began to melt, slowly revealing a land scoured and laid bare by the glaciers. As the ice disappeared, it left a landscape of barren rock on the high ground, and huge deposits of boulders, gravel, sand and mud deposited by the retreating ice in the newly-created valleys. The Sutherland landscape of today was created first and foremost by these processes of glacial erosion and deposition.

Slowly at first, a few seeds would have blown in from the south and taken root; seabirds would have colonised the rich coastal seas. More and more plants grew – grasses, then shrubs, and finally trees – each contributing by its death to the inexorable formation of soil. As the plants appeared, so followed the animals – first the herbivores moving up from the warmer south, quickly followed by the animals which preyed upon them. By the time the landscape had reached this stage, perhaps 9000 years ago, the land was ready for the ultimate predators – human beings.

These first people were hunters and gatherers, mostly on the move in search of game, but gathering the resources of both land and sea as they travelled around. They probably rarely stopped in one place for long, except perhaps near the coast in the springtime, when the only certain food supply would have come from the sea in the form of fish and shellfish. Because of this, signs of their passing are few and difficult to recognise, and it is only with luck, or through the disturbance of sand dunes in a storm, that sites of this period are found. This was known as the *Mesolithic* or Middle Stone Age.

In Sutherland, these sites are few and far between. The great midden of broken shells and animal bones within the great cave at Smoo may have begun to accumulate at that time, but all of what we can see today is later in date. Other shell middens, possibly of this period, are occasionally exposed near the coast only to disappear again. For the visitor, there is nothing much to see – but keep your eyes open, and report anything you *do* find to the Regional Archaeologist.

THE NEOLITHIC PERIOD

About 4000 BC to about 2000 BC

Around 4000 BC, new settlers arrived in Sutherland either
from the south, via the west coast, or directly from
continental Europe across the North Sea. Bringing with them
a tradition begun thousands of years before in the Middle
East, but only now reaching the north of Scotland, these
settlers were the first farmers. They grew crops, domesticated
and improved from wild cereals and other plants, and kept
animals bred from wild ancestors in the same way. These
enabled them to live settled lives although they would have
supplemented their diet by hunting – or perhaps by trading
with the already native Mesolithic peoples.

Such stability had a profound effect. They were not only
able to build permanent homes, but make a wide range of
objects that would have been useless to their predecessors -
heavy tools, fragile pottery, furniture and so on. The coming
of the farmers represents the beginning, in Sutherland, of the
Neolithic or New Stone Age, and despite the advance of
settled living they still used only wood, stone, bone and other
natural materials for their tools and weapons. One great leap
forward was the introduction of woven clothes – light, warm
and easily replaceable from the wool of their domestic sheep
or goats.

In order to create space for cultivation in Sutherland's
wooded landscape they would have created clearings by
felling the trees with their stone axes and using every part of
them for building houses, making tools, and providing fire for
heat and cooking. The stumps would have been burnt or dug
out, and crops planted. This is what we know today as 'slash
and burn' agriculture, and it would have meant that, without
careful fertilisation of the ground, it would soon have become
useless – so another clearing was made and they began again.
The forest cover would have decreased quickly as their
numbers grew.

It is possible that these Neolithic farmers built their houses
almost entirely of wood and, in consequence, there are none

recognisable in Sutherland today. What do survive are their huge and remarkable *chambered cairns*. These vast burial cairns are stunning in their size and complexity, and as many are built in prominent places – on top of ridges or low hills – they are highly visible, and would have acted as central points around which the social and religious life of the settlements revolved.

They appear to have been used over a very long period of time, and probably by the whole community. Some may have been used over and over again for 1500 years or more. Many were changed, altered and developed from small, round cairns, into immensely elongated 'long cairns' of which Sutherland has some of the finest. There are many chambered cairns of this period in Sutherland, some now much denuded, and the list below gives only the best examples. Many others are shown on the Ordnance Survey 1:50,000 Landranger maps, and can easily be visited should you feel inclined. Remember to ask permission before going, and treat the countryside, the animals, and farmer's gates and fences with respect.

One other type of monument sometimes survives in recognisable form from the Neolithic period. These are the *henges* – flat, circular enclosures built for religious purposes. They were built by digging a circular ditch around the central area, and using the material to build a bank on the *outside* – and thus clearly not defensive. These mostly very small sites suggest a very local function, rather than temples for a wide area such as that at Stonehenge or the Ring of Brodgar in Orkney. Note that the *henge* refers only to the earthworks, and those which have stone circles or other features have had them added at a later date.

THE BRONZE AGE

About 2000 BC to about 500 BC

The next 'Age', the Bronze Age, would have differed very little in terms of the day to day life of the people, who were still subsistence farmers. However, three important changes meant that this period is recognisably different in the archaeological record.

First, of course, was the acquisition of the new technology of metal-working, first in copper, then quickly the more complex manufacture of bronze alloy. The technology spread into Sutherland both from the south and from the continent, initially in the form of trader/metal-workers who would have been selling the new idea and searching for sources of ores. One of the earliest styles of bronze flat axe is named after a hoard of axes and other objects which were found by the shore of Loch Migdale, near Bonar Bridge.

The advantages of metal were considerable. Cutting tools could be more varied and could easily be resharpened simply by honing. Old tools could be re-smelted and the metal used again. Against this was the rarity of the raw materials, and bronze tools would have been both expensive and prized.

The second major change was in religious practice and in the treatment of the dead. Burial was now for individuals, each in a small pit or stone-lined 'cist' or coffin, sometimes, but not always, under a much smaller stone cairn than the great monuments of the Neolithic. Standing stones became important and were added to henges or set up singly or in complex groups as circles or rows. These monuments have a religious basis, but were also clearly designed to measure the movements of sun, moon and stars – most fundamentally to mark the year into divisions which would allow a farming community to plan its year more accurately in the absence of calendars and clocks.

The Sutherland climate is an unpredictable one, and this would help the farmers to avoid planting seed during a false spring, for instance, when they would be damaged or destroyed by unexpected frosts.

There are many standing stones in Sutherland, and some may once have formed part of more complex monuments now fallen or removed. When you visit, try to see them in their landscape setting, and imagine what they might have been used for, 4000 years ago.

The third, and in some ways the most important change – to the farmers at least – was the steadily deteriorating climate. In the Neolithic, the climate of Sutherland had been rather warmer and drier than today, and the area had been densely wooded. About 1500 BC or thereabouts, it became slowly cooler and wetter. The tree cover, already much diminished in the search for farm land, became thinner still. Wood would have become harder to come by, and more precious as a fuel resource. The response was to begin to build in stone – of which Sutherland has plenty!

For this reason, the houses of the time are still visible. All over Sutherland are the remains of circular house foundations known as 'hut circles', often surrounded by vague traces of the cultivated land which surrounded them. All that now remains visible are low, circular walls enclosing areas which vary from 5 or 6 metres in diameter up to as much as 15 metres or occasionally even more. Some are built on level ground. Others may be 'scooped' into the hillside, but most have a common feature – the gap in the wall which marks the position of the door almost always points roughly towards the south-east. As this is at 90° to the prevailing wind it would have diminished draughts and kept the houses warmer.

Excavation of some of these reveals that although there are variations, each would have had a pitched roof supported by the walls and by rings of vertical posts. A hearth sat in the middle of the floor. As they were dark places, most would have had paved areas outside, where much of the work was done.

Hut circles are often found in groups of two or three, but villages with as many as thirty or more are known. These are marked on the Ordnance Survey maps as 'settlement'. Often, those that survive are high on the hillsides on what was better drained ground. Perhaps many of those which lay in the valley bottoms have long been removed by later farmers. Not all are Bronze Age – huts of this type may have been used for 2000 years or more – some are later, and others may even prove to belong to the Neolithic!

Associated with the huts are the remains of their fields. In some instances, small rectangular fields defined by stony banks are still visible. Elsewhere, look out for scatters of stony mounds – 'field clearance cairns'.

THE IRON AGE

About 500 BC to 500 AD

This period is usually referred to as the Iron Age although again the real economic change is only in terms of technology – the people still farmed the same crops and animals in much the same way. Ironworking is more difficult, but the raw material is abundant in Sutherland in the form of bog iron. Look into almost any soil profile in the area – along new road cuttings for example – and you are likely to see, not far beneath the surface, a rather uneven, hard, reddish band. This is where iron salts gather as they leach from the soil in Sutherland's cool, moist climate, and gather as a deposit known as 'iron pan'. It is extremely rich and easy to gather. Metal tools of even better quality than bronze would have become affordable and accessible to everyone.

More obviously, the remains of this period indicate much more conflict between people, and this is the high period of defensive sites, most famously in the form of brochs and duns. Throughout Sutherland, people began to protect themselves by building thicker and higher walls, and by building them in more and more inaccessible places – on rocky hilltops, coastal promontories, or protected by water. Let us look at the variations in turn.

Perhaps the most well-known are the brochs. Based on the best surviving examples at Mousa in Shetland, Carloway on Lewis and Glenelg near Kyle of Lochalsh, they are seen as tall, windowless towers – precursors of the Medieval castle – with only a single, low entrance. Most have guard chambers opening from the narrow entrance passage, and many have cells built into the thickness of the wall, where there is often a staircase leading to upper levels, but by no means all need have been as high as those mentioned above. More sites will need to be excavated before we can be sure how varied these dramatic and important sites really were. Perhaps the principal problem in understanding the brochs is that of the roof. Were they roofed, and if so, how? We shall look at this again, later.

Next, and in many ways similar in construction, are the duns. While the brochs lie mainly in the north and east of Sutherland, the west coast is the home of the duns. Shaped to fit the site on which they were built, duns show the same features of thick walls, narrow entrances, and dramatic positions with natural defences. A number share the intra-mural passages associated with brochs. Some exhibit the phenomenon known as vitrification – walls once held together by a timber frame that was later set on fire, either by accident or through attack, and which burned until the very rock itself melted and fused into a solid mass. Whatever their ancestry may be, they represent an enormously varied class of structure linked by their small size and defensibility. We shall examine some of these in more detail later in this volume.

Still on defensive works, crannogs are generally held to have their origins in this period, although some can be seen, as in Ireland, to have been in use as late as the Medieval period. A crannog is an artificial island in a loch or sea loch, sometimes linked to the shore by a causeway, which was usually built below the water level. They are defensible against other people and wild animals, they take up no useful agricultural land, and they have both a constant supply of water, and perhaps other food on their doorstep. It is a mystery why such ideal structures are not more prolific, and there are probably two main reasons for this. First, many must now lie under water and are invisible; there is a need for an active programme of survey. Secondly, there must have been widespread use of *natural* islands. Why build when there is one ready made? Much more investigation is needed.

Other variations of defended sites bear different names. *Wheelhouses* are fairly common in the Western Isles, and are related to the galleried dwellings, or *wags*, of Caithness. Both appear to follow brochs in time, and indeed many have been built on and from the ruins of earlier structures. Sutherland's only true 'wheelhouse' sits at high altitude above Loch Eriboll – an oddity in an even odder situation. The *wags*, from the Gaelic 'little cave', extend from their Caithness heartland just over the border into Sutherland, especially on the east side.

Finally, hill-forts, common throughout more southerly parts of Scotland and in England, may be entirely absent from Sutherland. While there are several marked on the Ordnance Survey Maps, particularly in the east of the county, these seem because of their altitude or exposed position to be more likely to have been built as hilltop enclosures under the more amenable climate of the Neolithic or Bronze Age. Until they are examined through excavation, this can only be an opinion.

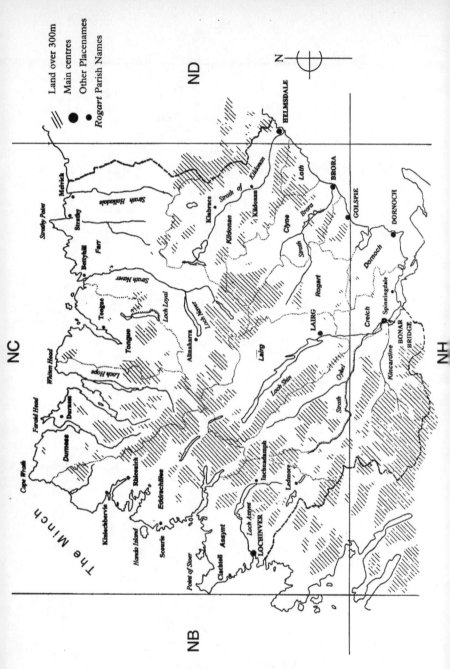

1. Sutherland, physical

THE GAZETTEER

Although the archaeology of Sutherland is concentrated mainly along the coastal strip or the sides of the main valley systems, some of the sites are difficult to find, some involve a serious trek across difficult country needing proper footwear and equipment, some can be dangerous in difficult weather, and a few are just not worth the effort! Because of this, the gazetteer describes a selection in detail, while the next best are simply listed. This is by no means a complete list, however, and if the visitor wants to explore *all* the sites in a particular area, he or she is recommended to consult the Highland Sites and Monuments Record in Inverness which contains full details of all of the recorded sites throughout the area.

This is a personal list, designed to introduce the visitor to a few favourites, while avoiding (generally speaking) the need to walk huge distances across quaking peat bogs, climb steep hills, get too near the edges of dangerous cliffs, or, indeed, have to be overburdened by the need for climbing boots and survival gear. Most can be visited with relative ease, and where there is a measure of effort involved, this is pointed out. For those who want to stretch themselves a bit more – do it on your own!

Stray archaeological finds – and there are many – are not touched upon unless they come from the described sites. Many of these can be seen in the National Museum of Scotland in Edinburgh, some are held in Inverness Museum, but any visitor to Sutherland should not miss the collection at the Dunrobin Castle Museum, Golspie, where many wonderful items from the Neolithic onwards are on display – many found last century by the Reverend Joass, an indefatigable seeker into Sutherland's past.

If a particular topic is not discussed in detail, or indeed missed out altogether, this simply reflects the huge wealth of archaeological remains in Sutherland. An appendix is provided to help follow up on points or areas of interest through the Highland Sites and Monuments Record and the various museums.

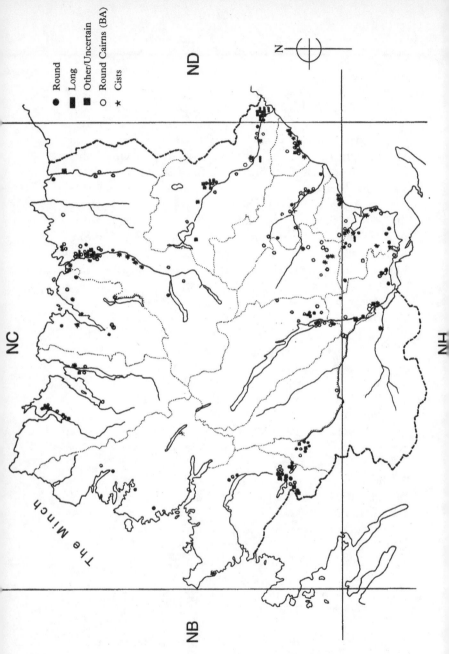

2. Distribution of Funerary Monuments

BURIAL MONUMENTS

Chambered Cairns

Cairns with identifiable burial 'chambers' rather than mere
cists are considered Neolithic in date. They are often
associated with more simple cairns, often containing cists,
attributed to the early Bronze Age. The best examples of the
chambered cairns (Map 2) are as follows:

Cnoc Chaornaidh, Kincardine
NC 2990 0841

One of a large group which stretches up past Loch Borrolan
and Ledmore to Loch Assynt and beyond, the site lies on the
hillside to the NE of the A837 near the turn-off to Benmore
Lodge. Its shape is slightly uncertain – circular, or perhaps
heel-shaped – as most of the cairn has been removed. Part of
the passage and a simple polygonal chamber defined by six
slabs and two portal stones remain. There is another round
cairn, perhaps later, nearby at NC 3013 0913.

Cnoc Chaornaidh, Kincardine
NC 3032 0793

Not far away is another cairn with much of its covering
removed, but with the main elements of the chamber visible.
Here, a very short (1 m) passage leads into a two-part
chamber divided by two transverse portal stones. The outer
chamber may have been added here, by converting part of an
originally longer passage into a second chamber. This cairn,
too, may be heel-shaped rather than round.

Allt Eileag, Kincardine
NC 3135 0794

This site lies close to the previous examples, and is more
certainly heel-shaped, probably with a forecourt enclosed by
short, horned extensions of the cairn adjacent to the entrance.
Flats slabs on the summit are corbel stones, and although the
roof has partly collapsed, chamber and passage are probably
essentially intact. Unlike the others, the cairn material has
been little disturbed.

Strathseasgaich, Kincardine
NC 3002 1028

A visit to this round cairn involves a good deal of effort. However, it is in reasonable repair, with the 15-metre diameter cairn clearly defined, as is the two-part chamber – the inner compartment almost circular. It lies at an altitude of over 200m overlooking Loch Ailsh, and is best approached along the track to Benmore Lodge and striking off into the hill before reaching the loch.

Loch Borrolan West, Ledmore, Assynt
NC 2603 1114

Between the loch and the road stand the much-robbed remains of a round cairn. Still some two metres high, the east side has been mostly removed. The passage has gone, and four slabs which appear to mark the outer part of a two-compartment chamber – judging by their off-centre position – look almost as if they are in a forecourt. The inner part of the chamber may well survive relatively intact.

Loch Borrolan East, Ledmore, Assynt
NC 2624 1118

Almost lost amongst the heather on the hillside, this round cairn has a polygonal chamber constructed of upright slabs with dry-walling in between. A small, roofed recess opens off the north side. The stone-filled passage has two surviving lintels and opens from the SE side of the cairn. A horn-like projection noted by Henshall may be fortuitous.

Loch Borrolan, Ledmore, Assynt
NC 2655 1104

A third round cairn above Loch Borrolan is much the same size, but although it has a central depression, there is no trace of a chamber, or indeed of a cist. Its proximity to the others suggests that this otherwise well-preserved site might conceal a chamber.

Ledbeg 'A', Assynt
NC 2343 1314

A longish, rough walk from the A 835 gets you to the two

Ledbeg cairns. 'A' is small and indefinite, and perhaps a later, unchambered cairn. There are, however, faint traces of two horn-like appendages which suggest a Neolithic date.

Ledbeg 'B', Assynt
NC 2343 1314

Having seen Ledbeg 'A', this is a much easier site to understand. Considerably larger, there is also much more to see. Portal stones mark the start of the entrance passage, which leads to two further protruding slabs with a lintel above them which marks the entrance to a two-compartment chamber. Both parts are polygonal, and separated by a further pair of dividing slabs. A massive back slab marks the inner end.

Allt Sgiathaig, Skiag Bridge, Assynt
NC 2341 2552

Whether ascending or descending the hill north of Skiag Bridge, be careful not to blink or you may miss this cairn! Missed by a whisker by road improvements, the remains of a simple polygonal chamber will reward the short, but steep scramble up the bank on the east side of the road. This is the northernmost of the group associated with the limestone outcrop.

Carrachan Dubh, Inchnadamph, Assynt
NC 2610 2176

Only for the fit, a visit to this cairn requires a rough walk of about a mile up the Traligill Burn, but the limestone scenery is worth the effort alone. The cairn is round, a little over 15 metres in diameter, and about 2 metres in height. A few upright slabs just standing proud of the cairn material suggest a passage and chamber is just tantalisingly invisible.

Ardvreck, Loch Assynt, Assynt (Figure 2a)
NC 241 237

If you can take your eyes off the romantic Ardvreck castle for a minute, you will find the remains of a chambered cairn on the top of a hillock close to the road. Excavated by Cree in

1925, only part of the inner features are now visible – the inner compartment of a three-part chamber and the septal slab which divided it from its neighbour – and now looking more like a cist than a chamber. This is one of a group of cairns which lie on or near the limestone which outcrops in this area and lends extra fertility to an otherwise rather barren landscape.

Kylestrome, Eddrachilles
NC 2188 3426
Built on a rocky hillock on the north side of the Kylesku Bridge is a smallish round cairn. There is no visible chamber or cist, but the monument is relatively undisturbed. Don't miss the nearby broch on its tidal island. Parking is available a short way to the north and should be used, as this stretch of road is fast!

Cnoc an Daimh, Badcall, Eddrachilles (Figure 2c)
NC 1667 4293
A rarity in this area, the remains of this round cairn are perched on a rock about 90 metres above sea level, with commanding views to the west. Four protruding stones at the centre suggest a simple polygonal chamber. Access from the main road is along a short stretch of rough track. Two hut circles lie close by below the cairn (see below, p. 59).

Badnabay, Laxford Bridge, Eddrachilles
NC 2187 4676
Whether driving north or south along the A894 between Scourie and Laxford Bridge, keep alert, or you may miss the remains of this polygonal-chambered round cairn half-hidden in vegetation between the new road and the old one to the east. All of the cairn material is gone, but fifteen upright stones clearly mark the position of the passage, antechamber and chamber proper. A keen eye will be able to trace the outline of the original cairn amongst the heather and bog myrtle.

Cnoc na Moine, Kyle of Sutherland, Durness
NC 3898 6609

Climb up from the road towards a rocky outcrop, just below which, on flat pasture, lie the much-robbed remains of a round cairn. What principally remains are the slabs and boulders forming a two-compartment chamber of some size, still with much cairn material inside. Not spectacular, but the walk is worth it for the views alone.

Torran a' Bhuachaille, Hope, Durness
NC 4687 5893

Follow the forest road down the west side of Loch Hope for a short distance to find a round cairn with a depression in the centre which probably marks the position of a chamber. A large, vertical slab is perhaps the end-stone. The site is not dramatic, but the walk is lovely. Carry on a little further, until you come to the remains of the deserted township of Arnaboll, where there are the remains of another burial cairn (below). Arnaboll itself is worth the walk.

Arnaboll, Hope, Durness
NC 4686 5801

To reach this, go through the forest gate west of Hope bridge and follow the track southwards along Loch Hope as described above. It is not a chambered cairn, but a large round cairn which may have contained a cist or other structure. Most of the cairn material is probably built into the stone wall which surrounds the enclosed sheep park of the Arnaboll sheep farm. On the hill above is the Arnaboll Graveyard, while higher still, the foundations of the cleared houses of Arnaboll Township can be found scattered amongst the grass and heather.

Tongue House, Tongue
NC 5926 5862

In the wood, east of Tongue House, are the much-robbed remains of a round cairn excavated last century and subsequently almost destroyed. All that is really apparent is the kerb of large boulders, defining an area about 17 metres in diameter.

Coillenaborgie North, Strathnaver, Farr
NC 715 590

Turn southwards from the E end of the Naver bridge along the Skelpick road and you can't miss the cairns just above the road on the left side. Continue to the quarry at Achanlochy to park, and walk back. Once thought to be two separate cairns, it is now generally accepted that this is a much-disturbed long cairn. The original form is difficult to make out, and the site is therefore less impressive than its sister cairn immediately to the south. Originally horned and about 48 metres in length, robbing and a cart track have reduced the site to its present condition. The simple polygonal chamber is now full to the top with a midden deposit of much more recent date – namely countless broken bottles and beer cans! Nevertheless, the view along both cairns – extending over 130 metres and more – indicates the magnitude of the monuments.

Coillenaborgie South, Strathnaver, Farr (Figure 1a)
NC 715 590

Just beyond the north cairn, and less than 10 metres from it, lies the impressive bulk of Coillenaborgie South. While much of the body of the cairn has gone, the original edge can be made out by following the remains of a kerb of upright stones extending intermittently along its length – some 72 metres. At the north end, two horns enclose a rather rectangular forecourt marked by six upright stones, the tallest of which stands over 2 metres high. The line of the passage, which led from the forecourt, is still visible over much of its length, and several lintels are still in position. An antechamber gives way to a main chamber of two compartments which is probably intact, although roofless, below the rubble. The single slab which forms the back wall of the chamber can also still be seen. The floor of the chamber lies some 2.4 metres below the visible wall-top. As you return to the parking place, have a look at Achanlochy township, one of those deserted at the time of the notorious Strathnaver clearances.

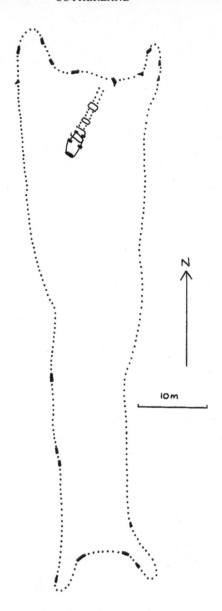

Figure 1a. Chambered Long Cairn (after Henshall),
Coillenaborgie South

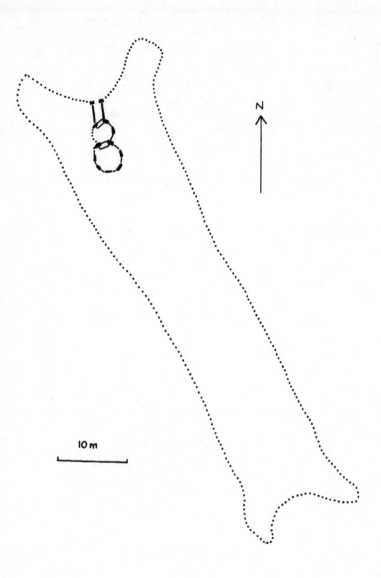

Figure 1b. Chambered Long Cairn (after Henshall),
Skelpick

Skelpick, Strathnaver, Farr (Figure 1b)
NC 7225 5672; NC 7249 5605; NC 7217 5635

Of the three chambered cairns at Skelpick, the most impressive is Skelpick Long, on the east side of the Skelpick Burn a little further along the same road. It is some 51 metres in length, excluding the horns which project from either end. At the wider, NW end, the horns enclose a forecourt about 16 metres across. The axis of the chamber and passage is at an angle to the cairn itself, and may suggest that an earlier, round cairn preceded the building of the long tail, as at Camster in Caithness. The two-compartment chamber still survives to a height of about 1.8 metres, but this is concealed by debris on the floor. The oversailing corbelling of the chamber, above the slab and dry-walling construction, is clearly visible. Lintels still survive where the projecting stones divide the compartments and at the end of the passage, and at a lower level. The original roof height of the inner chamber, when excavated in 1867, was estimated at about 3 metres, although the upper part had already collapsed.

Not far away are the remains of Skelpick South. While no trace of passage or chamber can now be seen, this exhibits clearly the short, horned form of the northern group of cairns. It is possible that the internal structures are still intact.

A third cairn lies nearby. Much robbed, the remains are now sadly obscured by a former rubbish tip.

Skail, Strathnaver, Farr (Figure 2d)
NC 7129 4690

Just east of the Strathnaver road, in a flat field, lies a cairn which has had almost all its covering stone robbed. The passage is not detectable, only most of a two-compartment chamber. The inner compartment consists of 5 upright slabs, the tallest about 1.8 metres high, with dry-walling between them. Two portal stones mark the transition to the outer compartment, which has now only one side intact. The setting, in a rather aged birch wood, is charming. Please be careful where you park when visiting this site, and make sure your car is clearly visible to other road users. Parking at the Syre junction, some distance to the south, is recommended.

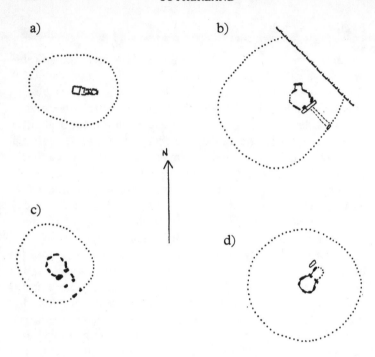

Figure 2. Plans: Chambered Round Cairns (after Henshall)
a) Ardvreck b) Kyleoag c) Badnabay d) Skail

Fiscary, Farr
NC 7311 6261
Two large cairns occupy the summit of a rocky ridge on the
north side of the A836 east of Bettyhill, and are visible from
some distance. The larger cairn is chambered, containing an
almost rectangular chamber subdivided into three
compartments by dividing slabs set in pairs, although only
the very tops of the structure is now visible. A larger cairn,
some 3 metres high and possibly quite intact, stands beside it.
The two are joined by a stony platform, and it is likely that
the two were amalgamated into a long cairn at some stage in
their development.

Kinbrace Burn, Kinbrace, Kildonan
NC 8757 2830

Probably the best of a substantial group in this area, this much-disturbed and overgrown short, horned cairn sits high on the hillside above the Strath of Kildonan near its head. The chamber consists of three compartments, each separated from the other by transverse slabs, and built of edge-set slabs with carefully-laid dry-walling between and above them. Most of the chamber area retains its roof, although at least one of the lintels is cracked. Please take extreme care if visiting.

The Ord South, Lairg (Figure 3. Site 1)
NC 5740 0559

Approach the site across the Shin bridge at the south of the village and follow the signs to the Ferrycroft Countryside Centre, from where follow the path up the hill to its summit. Little remains of this cairn beyond some of the slabs which define the position of the passage and chamber. This was probably the first cairn on the site, indicated by its prime position on the summit, later to be – perhaps – dismantled to build its replacement less than 80 metres away. Both this cairn, and the Ord South, are now part of the Ord Archaeological Trail which begins at the Ferrycroft Countryside Centre. The centre deals with the history of forests in Sutherland and their relationship with people from earliest times. A visit is recommended.

The Ord North, Lairg (Figure 3.Site 2)
NC 5733 0560

Just below the previous cairn, and unmissable! Excavated by Dr John Corcoran in the 1960s, the major elements of the cairn – chamber and passage – had to be backfilled for safety reasons. For this reason, all that can be seen now are glimpses of the massive lintel slabs which roofed the entrance passage underneath the huge pile of stones which make up the cairn. Note the stony 'platform' on which the cairn sits.

Excavations revealed a low, narrow passage some 4.5 metres long leading to a broad, polygonal antechamber, with beyond, a slightly larger chamber which was also polygonal in shape. The corbelled roof of this must have originally stood about 3 metres high. A wide range of Neolithic pottery sherds were recovered from the interior, including an almost complete "Unstan" bowl, a number of worked flints, a decorated bone mount, and evidence of at least two cremations.

The rest of the Ord Trail (Figure 3) includes a series of fine hut circles of varying size, a group of later, bronze age 'kerbed' cairns, and a large burnt mound (see below for discussion) rather obscured by heather. A guide leaflet or booklet for the Trail, with reconstruction drawings of some of the sites, is available at the Ferrycroft Countryside Centre.

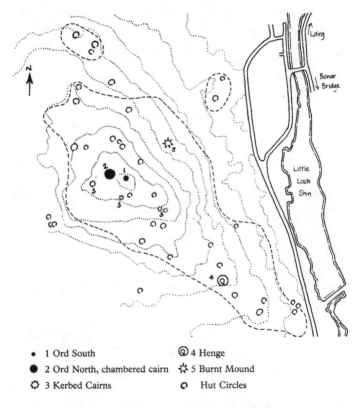

• 1 Ord South	◉ 4 Henge
● 2 Ord North, chambered cairn	✵ 5 Burnt Mound
✿ 3 Kerbed Cairns	○ Hut Circles

Figure 3. Monuments at Ord Hill, Lairg

Embo, Dornoch
NH 8177 9265

This site is included mainly because it is so easy to see – standing in the car park outside the 'Grannie's Heilan' Hame' pub in Embo village! Excavated by Audrey Henshall, the cairn contained two chambers and a number of cists. You will need a good imagination to unravel the untidy complex of slabs visible today!

Kyleoag, Spinningdale, Dornoch (Figure 2b)
NH 6628 9112

Recently cleared of trees, this site is worthwhile for the small chamber built off the main one, and the massive lintel which spans the transition from the passage to the chamber. Access is from the entrance to two houses just below. Park carefully, and *please* keep to the marked path to avoid disturbance to the occupants of the house on whose ground this lies.

Other Chambered Cairns:

NC 2382 1215	**Ledmore River** Round, chambered.
NC 2405 1464	**Cnoc Bad na Cleithe** Round, no chamber evident.
NC 2503 1464	**Loynemore** Round, possibly chambered.
NC 2538 5177	**Rhiconich** Round, chambered.
NC 3013 0913	**Cnoc Chaornaidh** Round, no chamber evident.
NC 3017 0818	**Cnoc Chaornaidh** Round, probably chambered.
NC 2489 1411	**Lyne, Assynt** Round, chamber visible.
NC 3115 0980	**Loch Ailsh** Oval, probably chambered.
NC 3170 0853	**Garbh Ath Chaoruinn** Heel-shaped, chambered.
NC 3665 6149	**River Dionard** Round, chambered?

NC 3715 6233   **Ach A'Chorrain**
                 Round, chambered.
NC 3733 6312   **Allt A'Chaoruinn**
                 Round, chambered.
NC 5498 5260   **Kinloch Lodge**
                 Round, chambered.
NC 5647 6305   **Dalvraid**
                 Round, chambered.
NC 6224 6010   **Blandy**
                 Oval, chambered.
NC 6737 5940   **Borgie**
                 Round, chambered.
NC 6876 6140   **Dun Riaskidh**
                 Round, chambered.
NC 7194 5500   **Achcheargary**
                 Round, chambered.
NC 7247 5687   **Skelpick**
                 Round, chambered?
NC 7274 5185   **Dun Viden**
                 Round, chambered.
NC 8299 0060   **Benbhraggie Wood**
                 Not much now to see.
NC 8275 1150   **Allt A'Mhuilinn**
                 3 internal slabs visible.
NC 8348 3217   **Carn Richard**
                 Short, horned, chambered.
NC 8690 3094   **Creag nan Caorach W**
                 Square, horned, chambered.
NC 8707 3094   **Creag nan Caorach E**
                 Round, chambered.
NC 8717 2915   **Kinbrace Farm**
                 Two cairns, originally one?
NC 8688 2935   **Kinbrace Farm**
                 Round, possibly intact.
NC 8754 2873   **Kinbrace Farm**
                 Round, two-part chamber.

NC 8821 6443 **Melvich**
Round, chambered (ruined).

NH 6715 9116 **Achaidh**
Heel-shaped, simple chamber

NH 7634 9000 **Evelix**
Round, chambered.

NH 7439 8967 **Clashmore**
Little remains today.

NH 7671 9673 **Cnoc Odhar**
Only the chamber intact.

NH 7411 9945 **Carn Liath**
Unreachable in dense woods.

Later Burial Cairns and Cist Burials

There are substantial number of large stone cairns, almost all of which are likely to be burial cairns – some perhaps even chambered – but where in many cases all that can be seen is a simple pile of stones (Map 2). Without visible evidence of what might lie within, or below, these are classified simply as probable burial cairns, whatever their size. A few have already been described above where it is *suspected* that they contain chambers, and are therefore likely to be of Neolithic date.

In some cases, a different form of burial is evident. These are the cairns containing 'cists' or stone coffins. This form of burial appears around the transition period between the Stone and Bronze Ages – about 2000 BC or a little earlier – when the so-called 'Beaker' people arrived from the continent, bringing with them copper and bronze technology, and new religious practices. Burials were now individually placed in these 'cists' or in simple graves, sometimes within or below a stone cairn (Map 2), but often without any kind of above ground marker. Often, the cists contain grave goods, mostly simply a decorated 'beaker' pot, specially made to accompany the burial, and less often other artefacts which can help identify the sex and/or occupation of the body. The following descriptions deal with the best of the cairns with cists, with a few cairns with well-marked 'kerbs' of boulders, and some of the isolated burial cists without cairns.

Burial Cairns with 'Cists'

Glacbain, Elphin, Assynt
NC 2231 1201

A somewhat remote cairn on the spur of a hill summit, it is both kerbed by boulders and has a central cist. It is small – only about 5 metres in diameter. The cist measures 110cm x 50cm x 40cm deep, with its broken capstone lying across it.

Sarsgrum, Kyle of Durness, Durness
NC 3792 6434

A much larger cairn, some 16 metres in diameter, lies about 350 metres NNE of the shepherd's house at Sarsgrum. Most of the cairn has been removed, exposing a cist consisting of three upright slabs and one fallen. The capstone, measuring about 1.5m x 1.0m and 20cm thick, lies on the top of the cist.

Allt a'Mhuilinn, Loch Hope, Durness
NC 4724 5770

Almost opposite the *Arnaboll* cairn (described above) on the east side of Loch Hope is a ruinous round cairn now half collapsed into the loch and exposing a cist. The cist is now empty, but the capstone and three of the side-slabs remained at my last visit.

The Ord, Lairg (Figure 3. Site 3)
NC 573 054

Within the archaeological trail, and below the two chambered cairns, are three round 'kerbed' cairns. The boulder kerbs are quite visible, if incomplete. These cairns may contain central cists or burial pits.

Invernaver, Bettyhill, Farr
NC 699 611

Amongst the extensive settlement of hut circles and their associated field system at Invernaver are a number of stone cists, wholly exposed by the removal of their sand covering by the wind. These are very easy to see, but as the river terrace at Invernaver is a Site of Special Scientific Interest, please keep away from the very fragile and easily-disturbed north end of the terrace and beware of causing any damage to the area whatsoever – or of interfering with the fishing!

Dalmor, Strathnaver, Farr
NC 7177 5509

Two much-damaged cairns lie close together, one with a central cist complete with capstone and a cavity to the north which suggests the presence of a second. The other cairn has only a single slab close to the middle which suggests a possible cist. These are most notable for the discovery in 1938 – once again by a road worker – of most of a very fine jet necklace and a jet button of bronze age date. The finds are in the Royal Museum of Scotland, Edinburgh.

Kirtomy, by Bettyhill, Farr
NC 7426 6276

On the summit of a ridge stands a small, round cairn 8 metres in diameter with a prominent kerb of large stones. A central cist was revealed by robbing of the site in the 1970s. It measures 110cm x 60cm x 60 cm deep. The capstone, if one existed, is not in evidence.

Learable Hill, Strath of Kildonan
NC 8922 2351

The cist survives within a cairn which has an almost continuous kerb of boulders. It was excavated in 1886, producing a cremation, some jet beads, and nearby, an inverted cinerary urn with an bronze razor not unlike that from Skaig (p.37 below). For directions on getting there, see under the Learable Hill Complex later in the book. The finds are in the Dunrobin Castle Museum, Golspie.

Dunrobin Park, Golspie
NC 8465 0070

The site is now hidden in an old gravel quarry in the Dunrobin woods. It was found and excavated in 1880, and was shown to contain 'the crouched skeleton of a woman; a complete beaker; 118 shale beads; 18 quartzose beach-rolled pebbles and three flints'. The finds are in Dunrobin Castle Museum, Golspie.

Kintradwell Links, Loth
NC 9300 0795

A number of short cists have been found close to *Cinn Trolla broch*, and may indicate earlier settlement on the same spot. None are visible today, but a number of finds, including a bone needle and a flint scraper are in the Dunrobin Castle Museum, while others were removed to Edinburgh.

Torrish, Strath of Kildonan
NC 9761 1890

A smallish cairn, about 5.5m in diameter lies on the hillside above Torrish on the E side of the Coulan Burn, amongst a great many others, probably clearance heaps. The cist was discovered in 1868 and finds, now in Dunrobin Castle Museum, comprised a splendid jet necklace and a leaf-shaped arrowhead.

Linsidemore, Strath Oykel, Creich
NC 5451 9991

Narrowly missed by the straightening of the road, this small cairn stands on a natural hummock. It was probably kerbed, and two stones on edge close to the centre suggest a cist. Excavation in advance of the road in 1995 revealed only a small fire-pit and two curious linear features. At the time of going to press a date for the pit is awaited, but is expected to be contemporary with the cairn.

Balblair, Bonar Bridge, Creich
NC 6007 9384

Here, a large (20m diameter) round cairn produced, in 1853, yet another bronze razor and a cinerary urn. There is now no trace of the cist.

Kirkton, nr Golspie
NC 792 991

About 500 metres NW of the cottages beside the souterrain at Kirkton (see p. 94 below), on the moor, is a denuded cairn with a central cist. The cairn measures 17m in diameter, while the cist, with no visible capstone, measures about 120cm x 90cm.

Embo Street, Dornoch
NC 8089 9138

A cist was excavated from 'a large tumulus' on Dornoch
Links here in 1867. It contained only a few shreds of bone
and a flint axe head. The capstone apparently carried
cupmarks (see section below), and in the bottom a carved
piece of sandstone was found bearing a curious incised motif
rather like a child's spade, whose present location is unknown
to me.

Other Cairns with Cists:

NC 5945 0742	**Savalbeg, Lairg** Small cairn, cist possible.
NC 5790 0988	**Cnoc Chatha, Lairg** Cairn and cist in forestry.
NC 5668 5142	**Druim na Coibe, Tongue** Cairn and cist.
NC 5649 5131	**Druim na Coibe, Tongue** Ransacked in 1978!
NC 6437 6165	**Alltan Dearg, Tongue** 2 cairns, 1 with cist.
NC 7399 5898	**Clachan Burn, Farr** Cairn with central cist.
NC 7206 5770	**Rhinovie, Farr** Cairn and possible cist.
NC 8788 0575	**Aultririe, Clyne** Cairn and two? cists.
NC 8587 0809	**Loch Brora, Clyne** Cairns and probable cists.
NH 5831 9917	**Alltnagar Lodge, Creich** Cairn and intact cist?
NH 6166 9220	**Carn an Fhitich, Creich** Cairn, no cist visible.

Burial Cists

As very few of these survive their discovery, only a selection
of those which still survive as visible monuments are
described. A further selection of cists are mentioned from

which important artefacts have been recovered.

Bealach Lice, Loch More, Eddrachilles
NC 3357 3628

At the bottom of a gravel pit close to the road are three remaining stones from a 'beaker' short cist which was discovered by a road worker at the top of the hillock in 1967. The fine beaker, decorated from rim to base with comb impressions, is now in the Royal Museum of Scotland, Edinburgh. No sign of a body was noted at the time of discovery.

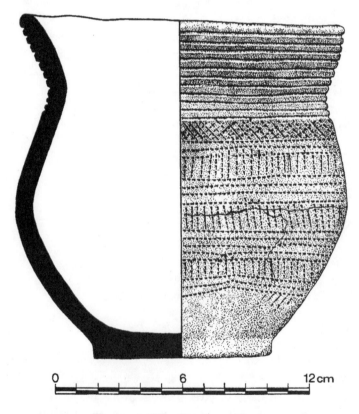

0   6   12 cm

Figure 4. The Chealamy Beaker

Chealamy, Strathnaver, Farr
NC 7240 5017

Found during road construction, this short cist contained the burial of what was probably a man in his mid to late twenties. His position in the cist was uncertain, and there were no long bones present, and the body may have been deposited in the grave in an advanced state of decomposition. With the body was a fine, highly-decorated beaker pot (Figure 4) which probably contained some kind of semi-alcoholic gruel for the journey of the departed to the after-life.

After excavation, the cist was reconstructed outside the museum at Farr Church, Bettyhill. The beaker is on display inside the museum. A second cist from Strathnaver was found at Woody Knowe (NC 7027 4577), also with a beaker. A single slab protruding from the back of a quarry excavated into a glacial hillock may be all that remains of the site.

Muie, Rogart
NC 67 04

Although the location of the cist has been lost since its discovery and 'excavation' in 1867, it contained a single flint arrowhead and a pottery 'food vessel'. The pot has been restored and is now in Dunrobin Castle Museum, Golspie.

Dalmore, Strath Fleet, Rogart
NC 7136 0306

On an almost impenetrable whin-covered glacial hummock on the floor of Strath Fleet are the remains of a cist measuring 100cm x 70cm x 50 cm deep. Found in 1869, it contained a bronze spearhead which is now untraceable.

Skaig, Rogart
NC 7411 0340

Although its origins are now somewhat confused, a fragmentary bronze razor of middle bronze age date was reputedly found in a cist, apparently under a small cairn indistinguishable from the numerous field clearance heaps in the area, during construction of a dyke. The razor is leaf-shaped in form, and decorated with a pointed oval filled with diamond shapes with alternate rows finely hatched. It is now in Dunrobin Castle Museum, Golspie.

Grudie, Rogart
NC 7370 0906
Atop a slight rise in the ground, and partially enclosed by three huge boulders, is a cist of four flat slabs measuring 120cm x 60cm x 30cm deep. There appears to have been no covering cairn, and nothing is known of its original contents.

Smoo Cave, Durness.

Chambered Cairn, Skail, Strathnaver.

Clach Mhic Mhios Standing Stone, Glen Loth.

Ben Griam Mor & Beg, near Forsinard.

Carn Liath Broch.
Entrance passageway from the interior. Note the 'guard' cell
and door jambs.

Kilphedir from the air.

Broch, Grumore, Loch Naver.

Vitrified Dun, Langwell, Strath Oykel.

RITUAL AND RELIGIOUS MONUMENTS

In the Neolithic period, 'ritual' seems to have taken place around the burial cairns. The sole alternatives are a few small, circular monuments with external banks known as 'henges' (Map 3). Far from being huge and impressive structures like those in the south of England at Stonehenge and Avebury, these are relatively insignificant in size – although I am sure they were no less important to the people who built them.

By the early Bronze Age, new settlers in the area had changed the form of burial and expanded their range of 'ritual' or religious monuments. These are the standing stones and stone circles, the rare and enigmatic stone rows (Map 3), and a limited selection of a feature much more common in other parts of Scotland – cupmarked rocks and outcrops. Most of them are described below:

Henges

Henges are simple circular earthworks identified by their component parts – a circular area enclosed by a ditch which is in turn enclosed by an *external* bank, thus distinguishing them from defended sites, which would naturally have the bank on the inner side. An entrance, or causeway, crosses bank and ditch and gives access to the interior. Some henges have two such entrances, usually opposite one another. Sutherland has few certain henges, but some, I think, have been wrongly identified in the past, and there may well be more to discover.

The Ord, Lairg (Figure 3. Site 4)
NC 5776 0521
Just beyond the present limits of the Ord Archaeological Trail at Lairg are the remains of a possible henge. The monument consists of a circular area enclosed by a ditch with an external bank, and a single entrance across a causeway on the SW arc. This could be the remains of a small henge about 26 metres across the central enclosure. However, it is confused by having what is a circular hut of the kind found elsewhere on

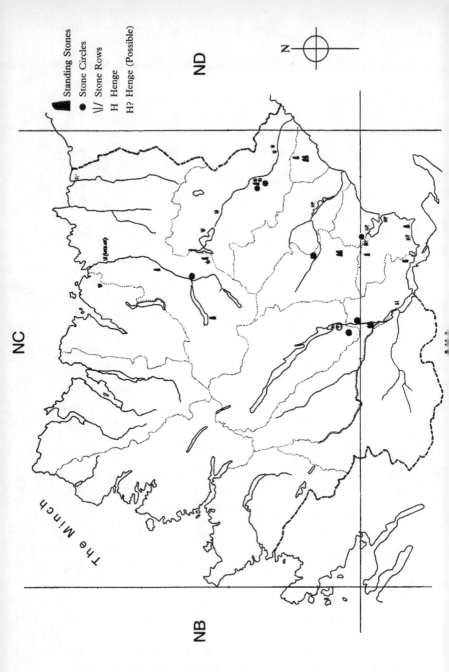

3. Distribution of Ritual Monuments

the hill within it, and there is a second possible interpretation as this having been a defended farmstead which only excavation could clarify at this stage.

Ascoile, Strath Brora, Clyne
NC 8309 1058

Immediately adjacent to the road and partly destroyed by it are the remains of a small, circular earthwork which has almost certainly been a henge. The remains comprise a tiny circular area, slightly 'humped', about 8 metres in diameter enclosed by a ditch and external bank. There is no evidence of an entrance causeway, although this may have been destroyed in the past.

Standing Stones and Stone Settings

Sutherland is not particularly rich in standing stones or stone circles (Map 3) although there are some striking examples, most of which are described below. Perhaps of more interest are the enigmatic settings of much smaller stones, set in multiple rows. These are unique to Caithness and north-east Sutherland and, as none have yet been archaeologically investigated, are little understood. Don't miss a visit to at least one of these fascinating sites.

Standing Stones

Learable Hill, Strath of Kildonan (Figure 6)
NC 8925 2349

A single monolith, about 1.6m high, stands amidst the splendid complex of circles and rows that top Learable Hill. This most important site is dealt with in more detail below. Continuity of religious observance is shown by a plain Latin cross, 17cm x 13cm, incised on its west face.

Achnagarron, Rogart
NC 732 049

Two standing stones lie about 30 metres apart, both with pointed tops. The taller stands some 1.5 metres in height, the smaller about 5 cm lower. Reputedly part of a stone circle, there is now no trace of other stones.

Leathad an Daraich
NC 717 349

Probably a standing stone, this site requires a very long walk indeed! About 1 metre high, it lies within a forest clearing where it has been preserved. The stone leans slightly in the peaty ground. Close by are a set of stone rows (see below), which tends to suggest it is authentic.

Clach Mhic Mhios, Glen Loth, Loth
NC 9404 1508

By a tiny margin only the second tallest monolith in Sutherland at 3.34 metres, it is nevertheless by some way the largest, and in view of its setting, I think the most impressive. It stands dramatically in the middle of the rather gloomy upper portion of Glen Loth, silent and mysterious. I have never failed to be impressed by its presence, in sunshine, fog, or thick snow. The winding drive up the narrow, twisting Glen Loth road is well worth the effort. Of the two smaller stones reported nearby in the First Statistical Account in 1798 only one can now be found.

Carradh nan Clach, Glen Loth, Loth
NC 9373 1273

A little way further down the glen, on a narrow ridge between two burns, are two further standing stones. One narrow slab stands to a height of 2 metres, while the other, square in section, is a mere 1.5 metres. Several flat slabs on the eroding slope to the SE suggest this may once have been a more complex monument.

Invershin Farm, Invershin, Creich
NH 5761 9673

Yet another pair of stones, those at Invershin Farm lie in the middle of an arable field. The obvious example is visible for some way, and stands to a height of about 2 metres, while the other, probably fallen, measures about 1.6 metres long and stands about 31cm high in a shape reminiscent of a hog-back. Don't miss the earthwork motte on the river-bank while you are here.

Clach a'Charra, Clashmore, Dornoch
NH 7164 8949

The tallest of the Sutherland stones and lying immediately adjacent to the A9, it just pips Clach Mhic Mhios by a few centimetres. A modern? drilled hole in the south face was interpreted by the Reverend Joass as being for the attachment of 'jougs'. Traditionally, it marks the grave of a Danish chief.

Dalnamain, Strath Carnaig, Dornoch
NH 7278 9858

Protruding through a low, straggling cairn of stones, probably field-cleared, in a walled sheep park, this fairly unimpressive stone (1.2m) was reputedly once known as the 'Swedish man's Grave'. Most of the stones on the east coast seem to have been attributed to a Scandinavian of one nationality or another!

Other Standing Stones

NC 4268 5599   **Allt Eriboll**
                   Uncertain standing stone in a small valley.
NC 6960 4603   **Woody Knowe**
                   1.1m high, but of doubtful antiquity.
NC 6694 5833   **Borgie Bridge**
                   Another uncertain stone.
NC 7808 8990   **Drumdivan**
                   A single monolith in an arable field just
                   outside Dornoch.

Stone Circles

There are so few of these that all the certain examples can be described in full:

Druim Baile Fuir, Achany Glen, Lairg
NC 559 029

Originally consisting of ten stones, nine fallen, ploughing and afforestation has removed all but three stones set in an apparent arc.

Twinners, River Shin, Lairg
NC 5824 0490; 5822 0493

On the banks of the river Shin are two reputed stone circles, close to one another. The northernmost consists of four boulders on the circumference of a circle, but a possible 'entrance' to the S, and its small size, suggests this may equally be the remains of a hut circle. The southern circle is some 6.3m across, but it is again unconvincing in its present state. Both are somewhat overgrown. Judge for yourself!

Achinduich, Achany Glen, Lairg
NC 5845 0084

There is little doubt about this double stone circle of which less than half now remains. Four stones of the outer circle and three of the inner remain. A steepish walk of about 400 metres, and sharp eyes, are needed to find this site on the moor. The tallest stone is only 1.3m high.

Clach an Righ, Strathnaver, Farr
NC 6793 3903

Please, *please*, don't try to cross the Dalharrold footbridge! It is old, and at the time of going to press, in imminent danger of collapse, so don't be the one to break it! Go round instead by the excellent forest road from Syre and drive or walk down the east bank of the river. The reward is a tiny stone circle known as the 'stone of the king', after yet another Scandinavian, King Harald Madadson, Earl of Caithness, who was reputedly defeated in battle here by an army under the Scots King William the Lion around 1196. The so-called graves of his men, scattered around him, are in reality nothing more romantic than field clearance heaps of Bronze Age or Iron Age date.

Only 7 metres in diameter, there now remain three stones standing, one only just breaking the turf, with a further three lying flat. A low cairn in the centre may well conceal a burial. The stones are impressive, with the tallest standing stone reaching just under 2.5 metres in height. The smaller is only slightly less large at just under 2 metres. The fallen stones are equally large, and the site must have been very dramatic when complete. The woodland setting rather enhances the solitude of the site.

Cnoc an Liath-Bhaid, Strath Brora
NC 7280 1016

Only the intrepid traveller will penetrate this far into Strath Brora, high on the hillside and well beyond the reach of the tarmac road! For those who do, the reward is another double stone circle this time with a better guide – a 2 m plus monolith marking the spot. There are still five stones of the inner circle remaining, with one prostrate, while the outer circle still has two upright and two fallen, with a arc of smaller stones on the circumference to the east. The outer circle has the edges of the stones towards the centre, while the inner stones have their broad faces to the centre. A most interesting site, and comparable with Achinduich even to its size.

Learable Hill, Strath of Kildonan (Figure 6)
NC 8916 2351 and NC 8945 2402

One certain and one more dubious example of a stone circle lies amongst the complex that is Learable Hill. Further description of the whole complex is given below (p. 48–51 and Fig. 6).

The Mound, Strath Fleet, Golspie
NH 7690 9908

The remains of a small stone circle of which three stones remain standing and three lie prostrate surround a central area which was partly excavated in 1867 to produce a cremated burial and an empty cist. No trace of the cist can now be seen. The shelf on which the circle stands was reputedly covered with numerous flint flakes, but please do not poke around to find them! The missing stone may be now built into one of the ruined houses beside the burn and just above the site.

Stone Rows

Allt Loch Tuirslighe, Borgie Bridge, Tongue
NC 6613 5874 (Figure 5)

On a gentle, peaty slope lies a setting of converging rows of small stones of which some fourteen appear to be *in situ* and represent at least three rows. Other stones are visible, but have an uncertain relationship to the monument. A stony mound, perhaps a small cairn, lies at the narrower, northern end.

Cnoc Molach, Badanloch, Kildonan
NC 7826 3516 (Figure 5)

Intermingled with a settlement of hut circles and their field system is set of 5 converging rows of small, upright stones, the tallest of which reaches only 70cm in height. Twenty-one of the stones appear to be *in situ*, with perhaps seven fallen or moved. As often at these sites, they are disappearing under peat, and this site was discovered only because the heather had been recently burnt. They may well be difficult to find now!

Leathad an Daraich, Loch Rimsdale, Farr
NC 7161 3486 (Figure 5)

A compact set of four stone rows, again converging on a small cairn. Thirty stones are visible, with another twelve located by probing just below the surface. The four stones on the ends of the rows at the wider, south end, are noticeably larger than the others. The site now lies in a clearing in a forestry plantation and might be hard to find, particularly as this is a very long way from the nearest road!

Dail na Drochaide, Strathnaver, Farr
NC 7205 5745

Now destroyed by ploughing, this was originally a five-row setting with eleven visible upright stones. No mound was associated with this site.

Ach na h-Uai', Kinbrace, Farr
NC 827 322 (Figure 5)

Somewhat larger than those above, this complex comprises

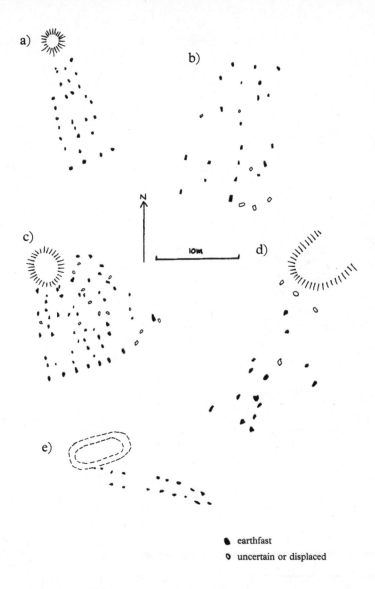

Figure 5. Plans: Stone Rows
a) Leathaid and Daraich b) Cnoc Molach c) Ach na h-Uai
d) Allt Loch Tuirslighe e) Torrish Burn

some 80 visible stones in ten converging rows, possibly a set of six and a set of four. At the narrow end is, once again, a small cairn previously dismissed as a clearance heap until recognised as a feature of the rows by Leslie Myatt of Thurso. The largest stones are again at the wider end of the rows.

Badiepullacher, Strath of Kildonan
NC 9549 1854

This ill-fated set of some 15 converging rows is now all but invisible, having first been partly removed by road construction, and more recently covered by dumping of material over the top of the remaining stones to form a passing place. Only two or three of the larger stones of the wider, south end are now visible just below the passing place. On the hillside above is a small cairn which was almost certainly associated with the setting.

Torrish Burn, Strath of Kildonan
NC 9657 1902 (Figure 5)

Only two rows this time, running almost east-west, and converging slightly towards the east. There are eight stones surviving in the southern row, nine in the other. As normal when the stones are slab-like, the long axes lie along the rows. No cairn is present here, and a small, sub-rectangular enclosure at the west end is unconnected.

Finally, while there are larger and more impressive sets of stone rows across the march in Caithness, that county has nothing to compare with the astonishing complex of stone rows, stone circles, standing stones – and indeed much else up to and including the early nineteenth century – that sprawls over the summit and slopes of Learable Hill. Because of its complexity, this site is discussed on its own. Be careful of access to this site, and avoid the bridges across the river Helmsdale which seem the obvious way in. Both are in very poor repair at the time of writing.

Learable Hill Complex, Strath of Kildonan (Figure 6)
Centred on NC 892 234

To my mind, this is perhaps the most interesting, if not the most impressive, of all the Sutherland concentrations of archaeological sites. You may have to walk some distance from Kildonan – check the access before you go – as the former bridge across the river near Skelpick lodge was recently removed as it was dangerous. Moves are afoot at the time of going to press to replace it, however, so you might be lucky.

Just above the railway line, a clear path leads upwards past the shepherd's house of Learable. The sheep farm which this represents was a second or third stage replacement for the huge township of longhouses from which the inhabitants were cleared at the beginning of the 19th century during the infamous 'Highland Clearances'. Unfortunately, these remains do not come within the remit of this volume, but a walk around the ruins and the crystal clear traces of terraced fields full of cultivation rigs should not be missed. Note the difference in these fields from the square ones around the shepherd's house.

Continue directly up the hill and head for the standing stone (p. 41 above) and its associated burial cairn. On the way you will pass through an area of field clearance heaps. Around the standing stone on three sides are the remains of three or four groups of stone rows.

This is by far the most complex set of rows so far known. Both to north and south of the standing stone, the tops of small stones protrude through the peaty soil and heather, and it may be necessary to walk about a bit before the rows become apparent. The emergence of the rows, in several different directions as you walk around the hilltop, can be quite magical!

You will see that some of the larger clearance heaps interrupt the rows in places, and so are almost certainly later in date – perhaps the religious significance of the hill had faded and it was thought able to be cultivated. In this case, the rows do not seem to be associated with any of the mounds or cairns, nor is there any obvious connection with the standing stone, which reputedly marks a viewing point for determining midsummer sunset.

† Standing Stones and Stone Circles   ○ Hut Circles

▦ Stone Rows   ♀ Cairns and Clearance

✳ Burnt Mounds

Figure 6. The Learable Hill Complex, Strath of Kildonan
(After R.C.A.H.M.S.)

Close to the standing stone with its enigmatic Christian cross, the visitor will notice two or three larger cairns. The largest of these, furthest to the west, is a burial cairn, which has been excavated. Continue west for only 60 metres or so and with care you will make out the better of the two stone circles. This now consists of 5 standing stones presumably *in situ*, two sunken and almost invisible, and two fallen stones. The tallest is only 60cm or so in height. They enclose an area about 18m in diameter. A mound within the circle and another just outwith it have been suggested as being burial monuments, but with the wide scatter of field clearance cairns in the area, this is hard to say.

Beyond the stone circle is another wide area of field clearance heaps and some long stretches of stony bank, with two hut circles on the slope below to the south. A later sub-rectangular enclosure lies in their midst.

Turn north now and skirt the boggy patch on its west side. This will bring you into another large area of field clearance heaps and stony dykes. At least three hut circles are visible amongst them. Go through this complex and head back towards the river, veering slightly south towards the 18th century township remains. If you are very lucky you might find the site of the other, much less certain, stone circle at NC 8945 2402. Lying on top of a slight rise in the ground, there are three stones close together, which if these were part of a stone circle, would have enclosed an area of about 14 metres. One of the stones bears an incised ring about 15cm across, with below it, four cupmarks of varying clarity.

Finally, there are three more hut circles within the township at NC 8950 2372, and close to the southern arm of a small burn at NC 8972 2371, a burnt mound (see below). If you are still fresh, cross back over the river and visit a similarly interesting complex on the N side of the Ach an Fhionnfhuaraidh (NC 902 239), with a broch/dun; some 10 hut circles and their field systems, and with 18th century remains intermixed with those of prehistoric date.

Cupmarked Boulders and Outcrops

These are few in Sutherland (Map 3), and with one exception, relatively simple in form and design. All are described or listed below:

Lochan Hakel A, Tongue
NC 5619 5271

Immediately W of the road from Tongue to Kinloch and about 800 metres N of the bridge over the Kinloch River, at the edge of a gravel pit, is a large boulder partially exposed to the air. It measures about 1.5 x 1 metres, and on its upper surface are 18 cupmarks of varying depth. No other marks are visible, and the cupmarks do not seem to extend below the vegetation.

Lochan Hakel B, Tongue
NC 5699 5264

Rather more interesting is a second earthfast stone at the S end of Lochan Hakel. Here, a flat boulder contains 34 cupmarks of which 11 are surrounded by rings. Local tradition suggests that the marks were made by the 'heels of a fairy who lived nearby'! Please check locally if visiting this site as there is a danger, at the wrong time of year, of disturbing rare divers which breed on the lochan.

Lochan Hakel C, Tongue
NC 5620 5275

Close to, but a little north of (A), is an extremely curious and enigmatic carved stone which is a complete mystery, but whose proximity to the others *might* suggest a similar date. The stone is earthfast, about 1.9m long x 0.5m wide, widening to 0.9m at its N end. The incisions vaguely resemble a long-legged spider, and have no parallel in cupmark art, nor apparently to early Christian or Pictish Art. A true Sutherland curiosity!

Dun Creagach A, Loch Naver, Farr
NC 6016 3499

After two attempts, I have yet to find this one. It lies a long where from anywhere, S of Loch Naver, and close to a hut circle. On its upper surface are over 20 shallow cupmarks, two of which are conjoined, and a single 'ring'. It is a long walk if you don't find it!

Dun Creagach B, Loch Naver, Farr
NC 6012 3466

Not far away – and I found this one! – is another cupmarked boulder. Measuring 1.7m x 1.5m approximately is carries 65 or so cupmarks, some of which may be conjoined. Another hut circle lies 30m away.

Allt Thorrisdail, Tongue
NC 6657 6181

Another difficult site to find. About 1500m south of Torrisdale, on an east-facing slope, are two halves of a split boulder standing about 2m apart. Each piece carries cupmarks; that to the west about 20, along with several carved initials. The smaller, easterly boulder has 25 on its W side, and a single one on the other. None of the cups are particularly distinct.

Learable Hill, Strath of Kildonan (Figure 6)
NC 8948 2400

A single boulder bearing two groups of cupmarks; 12 at the SW end, with a groove-like feature, and near the middle a further 7 with two 'grooves' (see above and Fig. 5).

Dalchalmie, Strath of Kildonan
NC 9313 1976

A straight line of three cups are visible on a large schist boulder which sticks out like a sore thumb east of the Duible Burn on the south ridge of Beinn Dubhain. The rock is known locally as the 'Maiden's Rock'.

Duible Burn, Strath of Kildonan
NC 9247 2045

Perhaps the most complex of the cupmarked rocks in Sutherland, this stone was placed upright after its discovery in 1933. It bears 12 small cups and two large ones, both of these surrounded by rings, and with a groove joining them to smaller cups below. Five other cups have grooves, and there is a trace of a third ring near the present base.

Other cupmarks

NC 4117 1120	**River Cassley, Creich** In Dunrobin Museum.
NC 6347 3837	**Grumbeg, Loch Naver, Farr** In Farr Museum?
NC 878 020	**Uppat, Golspie** In Dunrobin Museum.

DOMESTIC MONUMENTS

Hut Circles and Field Systems

Of the huge number of sites in Sutherland – hut circle country *par excellence* – it is possible to give a description of only a few (see Map 4). They range from single, isolated huts with no clear evidence of associated cultivation to massive settlements of 30 or more buildings surrounded by extensive areas of contemporary field systems. Within these large settlements, of course, not all of the huts need be contemporary, and their extent was probably much less at any one time.

Look out for the evidence of cultivation. In the main, this is most evident as a rash of small cairns scattered across the hillside, where field-cleared stones have been heaped out of the way with a minimum of transportation. Amongst the heaps, larger open areas mark the 'fields'. At others, traces of *lynchets* are visible – small terraces running across the hillsides which mark the divisions between fields. At a few, the stones have been cleared into field dykes which, roughly speaking, define rectangular fields often measuring 30 metres in either direction. Once again, these differences in cultivation patterns are likely to indicate different periods of cultivation.

Without evidence of Neolithic houses, these structures are almost all that we have of domestic sites until defence becomes important in the later Bronze Age around 900BC or thereabouts. The wide variation in the size and shape of the Sutherland hut circles may also be evidence of changing style through time that, as yet, we do not understand. Some sites indeed may last well into the Pictish period, perhaps particularly those which have multiple rooms in clusters, and which tend towards an oval or sub-rectangular shape.

The selection which follows tries to isolate the best individual settlements from carefully-selected locations throughout Sutherland. Added to each description is a list of other settlements – generally consisting of three or more hut circles within an identifiable field system – as well as some more isolated single examples or pairs of huts in the

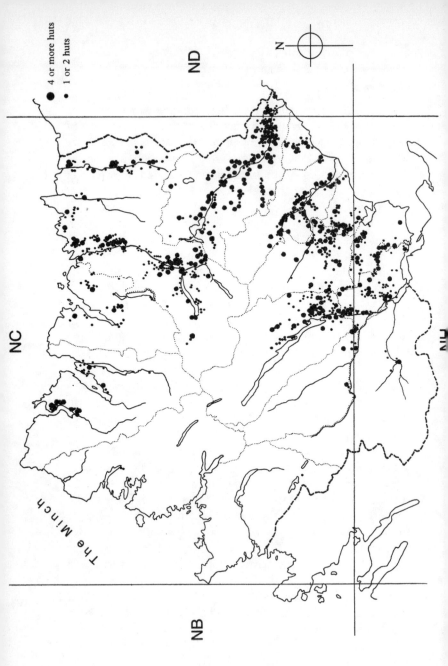

4. Distribution of Settlements

surrounding area. As very few of the Sutherland huts –
perhaps to be numbered in their thousands – have been
surveyed in detail, the descriptions may seem somewhat
vague. This should be seen as an opportunity to look for
some of the widespread variations of form which can be
encountered throughout the area, from simple circles, to
larger ovals, huts with expanded entrances, with sub-divided
interiors; with guard cells – an enormous variety!

Associated sites such as souterrains and burnt mounds,
although discussed later, are noted in the descriptions which
follow rather than individually so that the visitor has an
opportunity to look at a combination of sites which make up
the complex system of an early agricultural community and
its visible surviving remains.

Scourie, Eddrachilles
NC 160 440

To the south-west of the village of Scourie lies the small *Loch
Leathad nan Cruineachd*, around which lies a series of hut
circles with associated field systems and burnt mounds. The
simplest access is to walk in from the main road to the east of
the village, following the small burn which runs south from
the middle of the south shore of Loch a' Bhadaidh Daraich.

About 100 metres before Loch Leathad nan Cruineachd,
on the right side of the burn (NC 1628 4414) is a burnt
mound, one of two known which serve this complex. It is U-
shaped, and measures almost 10 x 8 metres in area and over
a metre in height. The open end, where the cooking pit will
have been, faces the stream. Although covered in peat, the
broken fragments of heat-cracked stones have been detected
by probing. The other burnt mound, of similar size, can be
found by retracing your steps for about 200 metres and
following a smaller burn, the Allt an Lochain Sgeireich for
another 200 metres or so, where it lies, once again, on the
right side of the stream as you walk uphill (NC 1657 4402).

On the way to the second burnt mound is one of the eight
recorded hut circles (NC 1655 4410). It is low and partly
obscured by heather, but measures about 13 metres across
from wall to wall. Facing slabs are visible on both the inner

and outer faces of the 1.5-metre-thick walls which expand to
some 2.3 metres at the entrance, unusually in the NW arc.
An internal compartment in the NE may be of later date,
while a crude lambing pen has been built against the inside of
the wall in the SW. The hut has its own, small field system
consisting of mainly of stone clearance heaps and possible
traces of lynchets.

From the second burnt mound, head uphill in a south-
westerly direction for about 130 metres to a second hut
within its own field system at NC 1647 4394. Much smaller
than the first, this measures only about 8.5 metres in internal
diameter. The entrance lies more conventionally in the SE.
Three crude bothy-like structures have been attached to the
outer wall-face at a later date. The field system is again
mainly marked by clearance cairns.

From here, walk westwards down to the loch. At the break
of slope on the small promontory jutting into the loch is a
third hut circle. This is a poorly-preserved example, about 13
metres in diameter, with a field system stretching along the
hillside to the NE. Continue, then, SW along the loch shore
and follow the burn to a walled enclosure just before the
road. Some 60 metres above this on the hillside is a fourth
simple hut (NC 4471 4378), about 9 x 8 metres with an
entrance in the east, with 180 metres to the NE a fifth, set
into the slope and now not much more than an overgrown
platform on the hillslope (NC 4484 4391). Yet another,
slightly oval, hut lies about 80 metres NNE of this.

Continue north-eastwards for about 400 metres through
the field system to the north side of the loch, where at the
same altitude is yet another hut circle (NC 1616 4425) which
is much more obviously oval, measuring about 15 x 10.5
metres. The walls are not obvious, and no entrance was
visible at my last visit under thick vegetation. Finally, turn
south towards the loch to another 'hut' site sometimes
described as a homestead. It is oval in shape, measures 13.5 x
9.5 metres internally, and with an entrance on the NE. The
shape and size of these last two, and their relative isolation
from the others, suggests that they are probably not
contemporary, but excavation would be required to prove

this conclusively. Turn east to the stream and follow it back
to your starting point. Other sites in the vicinity of Scourie
include:

NC 171 428   **Slugaidh Liath**
                2 huts + small field system.

NC 1665 4290   **Loch an Daimh Beag**
                2 huts just below the chambered cairn
                (see p. 20).

Kyle of Durness, Durness
NC 39 67 and surrounding area

This group is exceptional in that it lies on the Durness
limestone, which supports an area of bright green and fertile
grassland in the midst of the barren heather moors of the
extreme north-west. There are two main groups, with a
number of outliers, stretching from Balnakeil in the north
south to Keoldale. One focuses on Loch Croispol, while the
other lies to the south-west of Loch Caladail.

The first concentration lies between Loch Croispol and
Loch Borralie on a gentle, east-facing slope, around NC 388
687. Here lie some 6 circular huts in a tight group. Amongst
them lie several rectangular buildings of later date. The huts
vary in size from about 7.5 metres to 9 metres in internal
diameter, and in shape from circular to rough ovals. All are
relatively simple structures, with entrances, where recognisable,
in the east or south-east.

The second group is centred on the northern end of Cnoc
na Moine, around NC 390 660, and runs northwards up the
west side of Loch Caladail. There are some 14 huts in this
area, but in this case, with little trace of field clearance or
early cultivation. The huts vary in internal diameter from
some 6 metres to perhaps 10.5 metres, and are again circular
or oval in shape. Entrances again lie mostly on the eastern
side. One, at NC 3918 6593, has an expanded entrance
passage, while another, at NC 3918 6570, has its entrance
protected by a short length of bank at right angles.

Look out also for these other examples in the immediate
area. There are others, but these are perhaps the best. For full
details, as with the other areas, consult the Highland

Archaeological Sites and Monuments Record in Inverness.

NC 3880 6520	**Cnoc na Moine**
	2 huts + many field remains.
NC 3880 6540	**Cnoc na Moine**
	1 hut + extensive field system.
NC 3787 6695	**Loch Borralie**
	A small, single hut.
NC 3860 6659	**Loch Borralie**
	A single hut with field clearance heaps.
NC 3860 6680	**Loch Borralie**
	2 huts and some clearance heaps.
NC 3770 6670	**Loch Borralie**
	3 huts in eroding sand dunes.
NC 3763 6732	**Loch Borralie**
	2 huts in open pasture.
NC 3759 6710	**Loch Borralie**
	1 hut, lines and heaps of field clearance.

Altnaharra, Farr
NC 576 360 and surrounding area.

A small but accessible group a short distance along the Loch Naver road from the Altnaharra crossroads, forms the basis of a number of visitable sites in this area. Known as Gob Mor, the settlement consists of some 15 hut circles in two distinct groups. Four lie adjacent to, and either side of, the road at NC 576 356 and are scooped slightly into the hillside. All are slightly oval, and vary in size from about 9m x 11m up to 13.5m x 14m. A scatter of field clearance heaps and vague traces of terraces or 'lynchets' surround the huts.

To the north of the road lie a further 11 hut foundations of similar varying size to those above. All the entrances lie in the E or SE as is usual with these huts, which are somewhat masked by a covering of thin peat and heather cover. Three of the huts stand almost in a row at the lower end of the associated field system at NH 574 359, while the rest, higher up the hill, sit almost in a circle with the exception of a single site a little to the east (NC 5798 3612) which seems to have its own cultivation area, separate from the main one. The cultivation area is extensive, covering about 17 hectares, and consists of well-spaced field clearance heaps, a few lynchets, and a single stretch of walling in the NW.

Just to the west of the isolated hut, and between it and the main cluster, are the remains of a rather vague burnt mound at NC 5789 3614. U-shaped, it measures about 6m x 9m and stands some 75 cm high. A drainage gully which might once have supplied water lies just to the east.

Other examples lie west of the Altnaharra crossroads, and are listed below.

NC 534 360   **Cnoc Bad na Coille**
                Six huts, of which four are on platforms, with field system.

NC 517 373   **Barren Ridge**
                Two huts and field system.

NC 523 367   **Meaoie Burn**
                Hut with 5 clearance heaps.

Kilphedir, Strath of Kildonan
Centred on NC 991 190 (Figure 7)
Within about 1000 metres of Kilphedir broch are over 25 hut circles, mostly clearly visible on the hillsides. As some of this complex was excavated by Horace Fairhurst in the later 1960s, the additional available information makes this a splendid group to visit. Add the spectacular setting alongside the gorge of the Kilphedir Burn, the stunning views over the Strath of Kildonan, and the splendid broch right at their heart, and you have one of the best clusters of archaeological sites in all Sutherland.

The excavated group of huts lies on the west side of the burn at NC 990 193, but to get there you must first climb the hill through a whole series of others. Start from just west of Salscraggie Lodge and follow a rather vague path up through the remains of a former crofting township, when after about 500 metres – and having already passed a solitary hut-circle about 100 metres to the west – you will find yourself in the midst of a tight-knit group of hut circles and two cairns, one of which is chambered. The lower of the two is the chambered cairn, although all that is now visible is a group of large slabs protruding through the vegetation. Not enough visible structural details are visible at the second cairn to classify it, but it may also have been chambered.

Turning to the hut circles, the first group of five lies along a crooked line across the hillside, west of the cairns, and more or less on the 100m contour. A sixth sits a little lower downhill and close to where the slope falls away to the Kilphedir Burn. Two of the huts are more massively built than the rest, while the size varies from only 5 metres in diameter to over 12 metres. This variation in size and construction suggest they are not all contemporary. The associated field system covers over 14 hectares, and consists of clearance heaps and stony banks. With care, it is possible to make out small, rectangular cultivation plots measuring about 25 x 15 metres and defined by the stony banks. These are best seen near the western side of the settlement.

Having reached the stream course, follow it uphill for a short distance to a close group of three quite large huts set in a triangle. The first one reached is the best preserved. It measures 10 metres in diameter, with walls spread to about 3 metres across, but widening at the entrance to almost twice that size. This thickening of the walls at the entrance is a feature of many hut circles in Sutherland and may yet prove to be an indicator of date, but more need to be excavated before we can be sure. Pass through the entrance, as usual facing roughly SE, and look for a small opening on the inner side of the wall just to the left. This leads into a virtually intact souterrain. It is possible to go all the way in, but be very careful. The passage curves steeply down and to the right for some 10 metres and ends in an expanded chamber which is usually several inches deep in water. The passage itself is only 70cm wide and 90cm high at the entrance, so please don't get stuck. No-one should visit the souterrain alone!

Climb further up the hill to where the Allt Kilphedir divides, and follow the smaller, right-hand fork. After another 250 metres or so, you can cross the stream – with care – to visit a pair of huts set between the two arms of the burn. That to the west has a clearly-defined wall, marked by large

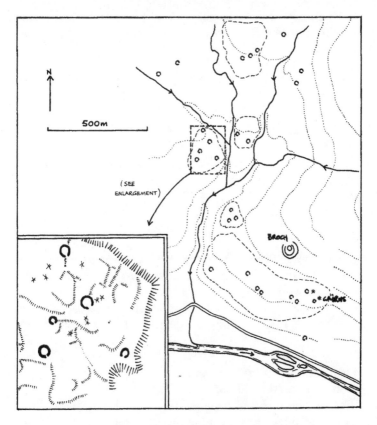

Figure 7. The broch and settlement at Kilphedir

boulders, almost 3 metres thick and enclosing an area about 9 metres in diameter. The entrance is in the SE. The other is about the same size, with a rough inner wall-face standing nearly a metre high. The entrance passage again leads through walls of expanded thickness, and is a little more than 1 metre wide. On the west side of the entrance is a depression which might mark the collapsed remains of a souterrain. Look carefully outside the hut and you will see that this hut appears to have been built within an earlier, larger one which was cut into the hillside. A few stones of its inner wall-face can still be made out.

From here, go uphill again, where surrounding the shallow bowl of the feeder burns of the Allt Kilphedir, are a further nine huts. Perhaps the most interesting of these are in the central group, at NC 992 198, where two are linked by rather obscure earthworks, with the eastern of the two having a 'hook' of walling at the entrance which provides a small forecourt to the hut itself.

Now cross the burns to the west side of the main stream of the Allt Kilphedir to a cluster of five huts and their surrounding field system which have been excavated (Figure 7). Two types were distinguished: types I and II, the earlier dated to around 500BC, the later to c.215BC. Hut 5, the only one occupied in phase II, overlay an earlier hut. This later hut had thicker, higher walls, with the now familiar expanded entrance. The field system, containing (a) field clearance heaps and (b) stony banks around cultivation plots, were thought to reflect changing cultivation methods associated with the two phases of occupation.

To get back to the road, follow the Kilphedir Burn on the same side and turn left for a 1000m walk back to where you started.

Dremergid/Garvault, Rogart
Centred on NC 740 065

The hilly ground, mainly croftland, which lies between Strath Fleet and Strath Brora behind the village of Rogart is stuffed with archaeological remains. Again, for full information consult the Highland Archaeologist, for all that can be given here is a taster of the riches of this area. Some of the huts here are very large and massively walled compared to some of those already described. Two of the most easily-recognised burnt mounds are also included.

Stop at the storage area for road materials near the summit of the road on the back way from Rogart to Strath Brora (NC 740 064). Almost immediately over the fence on the W side of the road and slightly to the S is a fine burnt mound. It is of classic U-shape and measures about 9.5 x 6.5 metres in area and stands about a metre high. Sheep scrapes on the side towards the road have revealed quantities of the shattered and fire-reddened stone which gives burnt mounds their name.

Less than 100 metres to the NW, near the summit of the hill, you should be able to make out what looks rather like a quarry. It is not, however, a quarry, but the complex remains of several hut circles of quite different construction and style. A second burnt mound lies nearby at NC 7388 0655, again with its composition revealed by scraping sheep. This is more kidney-shaped on plan.

The huts are most impressive and more clearly seen than many as the grass is usually close-cropped by sheep. The largest (NC 7384 0656) is massive, measuring 13 metres in diameter inside a hugely thick (3-4 metres) wall still standing up to a metre high. At the SE-facing entrance the walls increase in thickness to almost 5 metres! The whole is enclosed within an outer bank, which may have provided additional defence. Within the hut are traces of a curved internal dividing wall, possibly later in date, while outside the hut on the W side is a vague enclosure which probably represents the remains of an earlier, smaller dwelling. On the S side, and lower than the main circle, is another hut measuring 11 metres in diameter with an entrance in the SE. It is rather less substantial, and again surface indications suggest it might be earlier. The larger hut was originally described as a 'round tower' – no doubt on the basis of its size – and a bronze palstave is described as having been found here, although this may have been found about 600 metres to the south.

One hundred metres to the west is a third hut, only 7 metres in diameter within a more standard tumbled wall, but a recent visit by Royal Commission surveyors suggest there may be two other huts between this one and the other two, now visible only as flat, circular grassy areas with faint banks around them. If not simply field plots, these might very well be the earliest remains on the site. How revealing might it be if *all* the Sutherland hut circles were in closely grazed pasture, where faint traces of earlier structures could be seen?

Notice that the top of the hill is covered with field clearance heaps with occasional traces of low lynchet terraces and stony banks. Another hut lies on the N side of the road to Langwell just to the NE (NC 7407 0661). From here, follow a track which leads NNW across the moor from a bend in the Langwell road just below these huts, and head towards the summit of Creag Leac nam Fitheach, about 1500 metres away. Here are some 6 hut circles and a small kerbed cairn lying amongst scattered evidence of cultivation in the form of clearance heaps. That near the summit (NC 7347 0790) is about 9 metres in diameter, with an entrance gap in the SE, and also containing evidence of internal dividing walling. It is not clear if this is contemporary or not. That immediately SW of the kerbed cairn is slightly oval. It has a tall upright stone, about 70 cm high, flanking the entrance in the SE, while outside is a curve of wall representing either a field enclosure or an earlier hut. Another similar hut, this time with a curve of walling extending from the entrance lies a little way to the SE at NC 7343 0770.

Back down the slope at NC 737 076 is a group of three huts within a small field system. They are all oval in shape, and vary in size from 8 x 7 metres to 12 x 10 metres. All the entrances are in the S or SE, as is the norm.

While in the area look out also for the following sites, although there are a multitude of huts in this general area:

NC 7115 0758   **Achnahuie**
Hut circle + 3 later shielings.

NC 7210 0720   **Achnahuie**
Hut circle + small field system.

NC 748 046   **Cnoc an-t-Sidhein**
8 hut circles within two separate field systems + 3 kerbed burial cairns in the northern group.

Camore Wood, Dornoch (Figure 8)
NH 775 894

Within walking distance of Dornoch, Camore Woods contain both pleasant woodland walks and a substantial settlement of hut circles – some 25 in all – varying considerably in size and probably also in date. Rather than describe them all, try wandering through the complex and unravelling them for yourself. There are, however, a few interesting features to look out for. The diameter of the huts varies from as little as 6.5 metres to 14 metres – an enormous difference in internal area. The position of the entrances also varies enormously with three lying in the W or SW; about 10 lying in the usual E-SE; with the rest as far apart as N and S. A few cannot be determined. Two of the sites have extended entrance passages, there are three sets of 'contiguous' sites where the huts are attached to one another, and their position varies from the tops of knolls to semi-natural hollows. Many have stretches of walling attached to them. An altogether fascinating group, and well worth the walk.

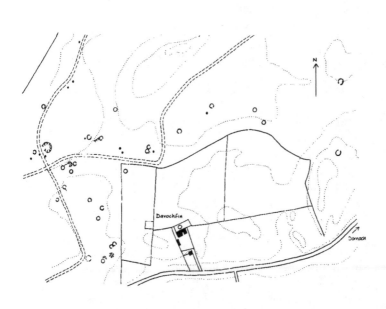

Figure 8. The settlement at Camore Wood, Dornoch

DEFENSIVE MONUMENTS

Brochs

The distribution of brochs (Map 5) is probably a fair indicator of the main areas of population at this period, although where they appear close together, some may be replacements for earlier examples which had simply fallen down. Brochs are particularly good indicators of local geology. Some, like Sallachy on Loch Shin, are built of good slab stone, while others are constructed of rough, rounded boulders which was the best material that could be obtained locally. Many of the minor variations in broch design may simply reflect the quality of available building stone.

Again, there are far too many to describe in detail, and those below have been chosen for the quality of the remains, their special features, or their dramatic positions. Most of the rest are listed, although some have been omitted because they are too ruinous to be worth visiting, or simply inaccessible.

Sallachy, Loch Shin, Lairg (Figure 9)
NC 5491 0922

This is one of Sutherland's finest brochs, although seriously in need of consolidation to prevent further deterioration. Visitors should take great care when viewing the remains, as the site is dangerous. Great care must be taken to avoid dislodging loose stones.

The broch lies in an uncharacteristic non-defensive position on a low hillock close to the shore of Loch Shin. The loch level has been raised for generating electricity, and it was originally somewhat further from the shore. The interior has been partially cleared in the past, and the outer wall faces also partly cleared. Outside, the walls are now visible to a height of about 2 metres, while inside, they are over 3 metres high. The wall is about 4 metres thick. Two corbelled cells open from either side of the entrance passage in the south-east, where recent collapse has masked some of the features. On the south-west arc is an opening leading to an intramural staircase, and a third cell, now roofless. Faint traces of a scarcement ledge, perhaps originally supporting a timber

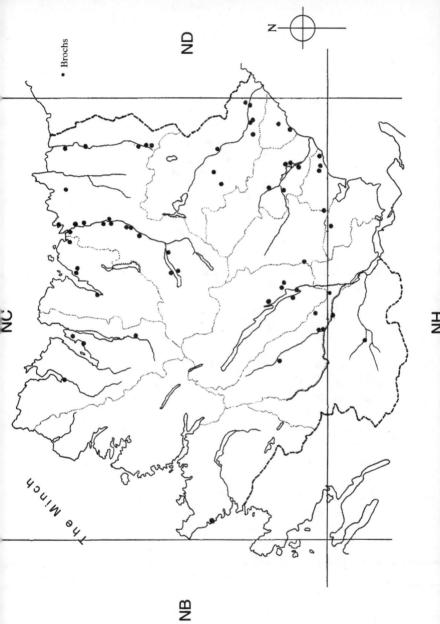

5. Distribution of Brochs

gallery, are visible not far below the present wall-top. There
may have been an outer defensive wall lying to the south-east,
while an enclosure defined by a stony dyke on the south side
may be of later date. Much rebuilding took place during the
Victorian period.

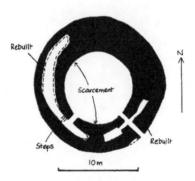

Figure 9. Plan: Broch, Sallachy

East Kinnauld, Strath Fleet, Rogart
NC 7438 0159

High on the hillside above the Kinnauld stone quarry are the
tumbled remains of a broch built of large, angular boulders.
While it is rather dilapidated, the inner and outer wall-faces
are clearly defined, as is the entrance passage – some 5.5
metres long with three lintels still in place. It is blocked with
debris, however. A cell opens from the passage on the south
side, while opposite is another which is linked to the interior
by a short passage. Traces of an intramural passage are
visible on the north side.

Another reason for visiting the broch is the fine view over
the complex little fortified site on the craggy hill just to the
west of the quarry, which is described in the following pages.

Backies, Golspie
NC 8345 0261

This is a little difficult to get to, and it is best to ask
permission from the estate office, but it is well worth the

effort. On first approaching the broch the visitor would be excused for thinking there is nothing there but an immense pile of stones! Once on the summit, though, there is much to see. Although the outer face is almost entirely obscured, the interior is visible around its entire circuit, after passing through an almost completely roofed entrance passage – in this case, without any 'guard' chambers. A large chamber in the wall thickness almost faces the entrance, with a short stretch of intra-mural passage also visible. A scarcement ledge about 2 metres above the present interior level can be seen in places around much of the interior.

The broch is further defended by an outwork which is much collapsed, although the wall-faces are visible in places. This may be contemporary, or could possibly be the remains of an earlier fortification on the same site. Several stone dykes radiate from the broch and appear to enclose fields, although they may be contemporary with the later crofting remains which lie nearby. The aerial view of the broch on p.XXX shows all these features very clearly.

Dunrobin Wood, Golspie
NC 8407 0176

Recently opened up by the removal of the wood which surrounded it, the nearby broch in Dunrobin Wood is perhaps less impressive. It sits on a hillock and is defended by a natural gully on three sides. The entrance passage with 'guard' cell is visible, and traces of the entrance to a staircase within the thickness of the wall on the north side. The outer 'bank' which encircles the broch seems likely to be the result of clearance around the walls, perhaps last century. The interior has been partly cleared out.

Kilphedir, Strath of Kildonan, Kildonan
NC 992 191 and area (Figs 7, 10)

This is a wonderful site. Set high on the hillside above the river Helmsdale, this very ruinous broch is surrounded by an outwork of massive proportions, and commands splendid views along the Strath of Kildonan. The rocks used in its construction are rounded, granitic boulders, which must have

been very difficult to build with and have surely contributed
to its present ruinous condition. In spite of this, the entrance
passage is visible, as is part of the intramural passage on the
south side. There is probably still a good deal of the wall
surviving, but invisible under the huge mass of fallen stone.
By far the most striking feature is the huge earthwork which
surrounds the broch, clearly visible on the aerial photograph
taken from almost directly above the site.

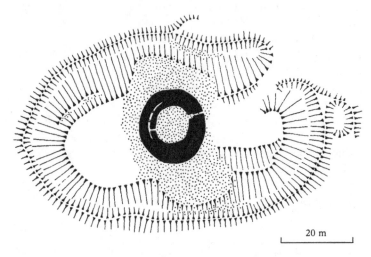

Figure 10. Plan: Kilphedir Broch

Upper Suisgill, Strath of Kildonan, Kildonan
NC 8875 2530

Although almost nothing remains of the broch itself, much of
it apparently removed just after the turn of the century, this
site again has impressive ditched outworks which make a visit
worthwhile. These would have been necessary, as the site
itself is not particularly well-defended.

The Borg, Strath Halladale, Farr
NC 8993 5095

Although somewhat altered since its construction, and
exhibiting few features of interest except the enormous

granite boulders from which it was built, this site forms a dramatic and unmissable landmark on its rocky knoll above the road. The short walk is worth the effort, and look out for the remains of rectangular croft buildings on the slopes between the road and the broch. Stone walls radiating from the site may be associated with either period.

Carn Liath, Strathsteven, Golspie
NC 8704 0137

Carn Liath is in the Guardianship of the Secretary of State for Scotland, and is probably the easiest of the Sutherland brochs to understand – particularly with the new interpretive boards provided by Historic Scotland. A large broch, it is particularly noteworthy for the entrance passage, extended through the later buildings which huddle around the main structure, the fine 'guard' cell, the intact section of intramural stair, and the well-tended grass! Be careful crossing the A9 – follow the signs and don't take shortcuts from the car park.

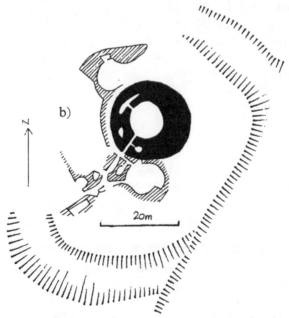

Figure 11. Plan: Broch, Cinn Trolla

Cinn Trolla, Kintradwell, Loth
NC 9293 0807

Those travelling by car will have to go some way to find a
safe place to park – please do *not* leave your car on the verge
near the broch. While a little overgrown and subject to
damage by cattle, the site is worth a visit for a number of
reasons. As well as the view along the endless beach, the site
shows evidence of passage, 'guard' cells and staircase.
Outside are the tumbled remains of a complex of later
buildings all contained within a wide ditch which ends at the
coastal slope. I would be inclined to check if there is a bull in
the field before visiting!

Dun Mhaigh, Kinloch, Tongue
NC 5523 5303

Another much-tumbled broch, but with one of the finest
views – over the endless white sands of the Kyle of Tongue –
in the north of Scotland! The entrance passage still retains
several of its lintels and a hint of a 'guard' cell, while the
intramural staircase still has eight of its steps visible. Dun
Mhaigh is unusual in being slightly D-shaped on plan, with a
flattened west side. The walls are still almost 3 metres high on
the outer face – but beware of the drop over the rocky cliffs.
On the easier approaches, the broch has been further
defended by outer stone walls.

An Dun, Clachtoll, Assynt
NC 0366 2784

The most visitable broch on the west coast of Sutherland, the
ruins of this site are under threat from the number of visitors
generated by the caravan and camping site nearby and at
Achmelvich. Please take great care not to disturb or damage
the remains.

A considerable portion of the building has disappeared
into the sea, as it sits directly on the edge of a low, rocky cliff
above the sea. What remains still holds much of interest. The
entrance passage has been extended, and that part of it
leading through the walls proper is partly blocked, but the
near-intact 'guard' cells opening from either side are visible

for the intrepid crawler. Note the triangular lintel above the entrance. This would have diverted the enormous weight of the walls to either side of the passage, and is a feature seen in several Sutherland brochs. On the south side, and only accessible to small, thin children, is a virtually complete corbelled cell within the thickness of the wall. The extended entrance passage penetrates as far as the outer face of a secondary defensive wall which extends from the south side and then swings away from the broch to the cliff-edge on the north side. Its is partly obscured by massive blocks of fallen stone. Between this wall and the broch itself there may have been small huts like those at Carn Liath and Cinn Trolla (see above).

Other Brochs

NC 3633 6200	**Ach'Chairn**
NC 4116 1121	**Creich, Glencassley**
NC 4459 5797	**Camus an Duin**
NC 4601 6053	**Ach an Duin**
NC 4686 0273	**Achness House**
NC 4701 0253	**Achness House**
NC 5273 1526	**West Shinness**
NC 5719 0679	**Ferry Wood, Lairg**
	A stony mound on a walking trail in Ferry Woods.
NC 5725 1116	**Dalchork**
	Recently opened up by Forest Enterprise.
NC 6036 5977	**Rhitongue**
NC 6046 3558	**Dun Creagach**
NC 6210 5875	**Dallcharn**
	Only a grassy mound.
NC 6300 0484	**A'Mheirle**
NC 6585 3815	**Loch Naver Inaccessible**
NC 6773 6185	**Dun Torrisdale**
NC 6926 4496	**Langdale Burn**
NC 6973 6097	**Lochan Druim an Duin**
NC 7139 5942	**Achcoillenaborgie**
	Ruined, but close to the splendid chambered cairns.

NC 7159 4657	Inshlampie
NC 7199 5140	Dun Chealamy
NC 7201 4732	Eilean Garbh
NC 7213 5269	Cnoc Carnachaidh
NC 7265 5188	Dun Viden
NC 7994 6266	Armadale Burn
NC 8462 0646	Carrol
NC 8550 0520	Leadoch
NC 8896 5752	Upper Bighouse
NC 8918 5338	Trantlemore
NC 9216 1887	Kilearnan
NC 9420 1220	Carn Bran
NC 9833 1816	Eldrable
NH 4564 9143	Croick
NH 5039 9853	Carn Mor
NH 5669 9098	An Dun
NH 7050 9903	Strath Carnaig

Hill-forts

Hill-forts, in the classic Iron Age tradition, do not occur in Sutherland. This may be due to a population density which was too low to support their construction, or simply that the early people of Sutherland were nicer to one another! Whatever the reason, the fortified sites which occupy hilltops are few and far between. There is some doubt about their classification as Iron Age forts (see Map 6), which should emerge from the following descriptions:

East Kinnauld, Strath Fleet, Rogart
NC 7421 0145
This is a most interesting and complex monument, if a little difficult to unscramble. A low summit, separated from the main hill mass by a deep gully and with steep slopes on the other three sides, is the focus for a series of defensive and other works whose relationship to one another is completely obscure. Immediately to the SE, the site has been impinged upon by a rock quarry, but after minor damage in the late

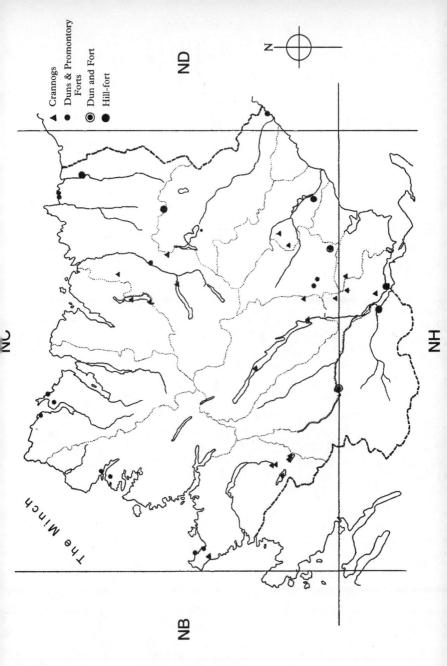

6. Distribution of Defensive Monuments other than Brochs

1980s, any further work towards the fort was stopped.

The outermost structures consist of a deep ditch and bank at the bottom of the slope on the north side, while a gully on the NE has been deepened to form extra defence at this point. Around the top of the break of slope on the S and E, where the rocky hillside begins to level out, are the very faint traces of a stony bank, now just above the quarry workings. Hardly strong enough to be called defensive, this defines the largest of the enclosed areas of the summit. On the west side, this bank runs uphill adjacent to a cliff edge to meet the outer of the two central enclosures.

Neither of these are of any real size. The outer wall is a low, oval bank of stones about 2 metres in thickness with no apparent entrance, but with outer and inner facing stones intermittently visible. Inside this is a second circuit of tumbled walling, perhaps 4 metres across, and again without any visible entrance. None of these features cross or overlap one another, so the sequence is impossible to reconstruct without excavation.

The general assumption is that the larger summit circle and the outworks to the W and N belong to a fort, while the inner ring represents the remains of a smaller defensive dun. Whatever the answer, the surface indications suggest a site which was complex, or long-lived, or both. A fine view can be had of the various enclosures as you walk farther up the hill to East Kinnauld broch (see p. 70), which may have replaced whatever lies below.

Duchary Rock, Strath Brora, Clyne
NC 850 048

Its large size perhaps entitles Duchary Rock to be described as a hill-fort, but its defences consist mainly of natural cliffs – the only built elements being walls which defend the easier approaches at either end. The walls are massive, however, measuring some 4m in thickness and still standing up to 1.5m high, despite rumours that estate workers had been seen recently removing rock to patch holes on an estate road! The area enclosed measures about 300m NW-SE, by a maximum of 100m in width – just under three hectares in area.

The interior is overgrown with peat, and it may be that the 'fort' should be re-classified, along with Ben Griam Beg (below) and similar sites in Caithness, as rather earlier hilltop enclosures and maybe with quite a different function. The site is at quite high altitude – about 230m – and must have been quite inhospitable in an Iron Age winter in Sutherland. A period before the climatic deterioration of the mid second millennium BC – and the onset of rapid peat growth – seems quite plausible.

Ben Griam Beg, Forsinard, Farr
NC 831 411

If this is an Iron Age hill-fort in the conventional sense, I will eat my woolly hat! Its claim to fame is that, at a summit height of 578.5m above sea level, it is the highest hill-fort in Scotland. Unfortunately, the climate at the top is positively sub-arctic, even in summer. The hill lies within the Ben Griams Site of Special Scientific Interest, which has been designated partly as 'a particularly good example of an Arctic-Alpine plant refugium'.

Recent work by Dr Ian Ralston has clarified many of the structural elements on this isolated hill, whose panoramic views extend all the way to Orkney, 60–70 kilometres to the NE! A visit requires a long walk, strong legs and boots, proper equipment and a considerable climb, so please do not attempt this unless you are fit, and preferably only in settled summer weather. The view from the top – if you *do* get there – is breathtaking (weather permitting).

The defences consist of a series of dependent enclosures stepping down from the summit, while around the 456m contour is an outer settlement of ruined walls which show massive distortion as they slip downslope under winter conditions of freeze and thaw. Amongst a series of stone dykes, which form sub-rectangular enclosures, are other structures which include, according to Ian Ralston: "stone clearance heaps, connecting lengths of track, small 'annexe' enclosures, and possible hut circles, some scarped into the slope". He also notes that some enclosures are "substantially infilled with peat".

Like Duchary Rock, and Buaile Oscar and Garrywhin in Caithness, the peat build-up on this site suggests a foundation date before the onset of rapid formation about 1500 BC. The vast area of featureless blanket bog which surrounds the hill also supports this theory, as there is no visible farming land for a long distance. At the Caithness sites, megalithic entrances also suggest a much older date than conventional hillforts, and this northern group may represent an important and as yet unrecognised type of site built during the early Bronze Age.

Duns, Wags and Wheelhouses

Duns

Without excavation, the dates of most of the Sutherland duns (Map 6) will remain something of a mystery. A dun is by definition a *small* fortified site, usually very heavily defended with respect to the area enclosed. Such sites may be varied in both their origin and function, and this is to some extent borne out by the wide difference in their structure, position, and to a more limited extent, their size.

Some sites appear to have much in common with the architecture of brochs, and there are some sites which cannot with confidence be said to be one or the other. Some sites, although small, seem to have more in common with hill-forts, serving as defended refuges for a larger community. Some again may simply be the homes of a farming family whose defensive elements may have been constructed against wild animals rather than human enemies. From time to time, evidence of more than one phase of defensive works could indicate either reuse of a particular site over time, or perhaps a change of primary function which required alterations or additions to the defences.

There are only a few duns of the classic west-coast style in Sutherland, most of the better-known examples lying farther to the south or, at their very best, in the Western Isles. The following examples cover a wide range of styles. Although generally assumed to lie within the 'Iron Age' – without excavation to clarify their origins and functions – they may well stretch from the early first millennium BC as far as the early historic era vaguely dubbed 'Pictish' and therefore chronologically beyond the range of this volume. Because of the uncertainty, however, they are included here.

Clashnessie, Stoer, Assynt
NC 0563 3157

Perched on the top of an isolated rocky summit which rises steeply from the shore, is a small defensive structure described as a 'promontory dun'. The enclosing wall is between 2 m and 3 m thick, yet encloses a roughly oval, flat area barely 6 metres long by 3 metres wide. Only the foundations of the wall now remain. The entrance appears to have been at the landward end, while on either side the summit is further defended by a deep chasm. Guarding the approach and some 3m outwith the wall on the SW are the vague footings of an outwork. The site is known locally as *An Dun*.

An Dunan, Culkein, Stoer, Assynt
NC 0419 9340

A second 'promontory dun' occupies a rock stack with a sub-rectangular summit at the north end of the Bay of Culkein. A thick 'blockhouse' wall defends the landward end of the promontory and, although its thickness is obscured by turf, it is clearly massive relative to the size of the promontory. The outer face survives to a height of at least four visible courses of square blocks.

It is reached from an inner promontory across a rock chasm crossed by a narrow rock bridge. This approach area is further defended by a curving outwork wall with a facing of boulders some 2.3 metres thick with a narrow entrance towards the south. Again, the area enclosed is small in proportion to the thickness of the defensive walls, and its date and function are obscure.

Loch Inchard, Assynt
NC 2272 5575

A small, rocky islet contains the very denuded and scant remains of a small, D-shaped, fortified enclosure or dun. It measures about 11 metres along its straight side, by about 8 metres across, and the wall, though now a ruinous rubble spread some 2.5 metres wide, must once have been strongly built. The islet can only be approached at low tide, adding to the defensibility of the site.

Loch Borralie, Durness
NC 3840 6753

Several visits to this site have done nothing to clarify its date or function, and it is included here as possibly being a dun. The walk to the site and around this area of Durness limestone, however, makes the fairly short walk well worth while despite its uncertainty!

The site lies on a rocky summit above the loch, and consists of a sadly-depleted circular structure enclosed by a grassy rampart of earth and stones now a little more than a metre in height and spread to a width of some 2.5 metres. The entrance is not visible. Its position suggests a defensive structure, but this should perhaps be described as a defended farmstead rather than as a dun proper. Its origins are further confused by the presence of a modern sheepfold and the foundations of several rectangular buildings, probably of nineteenth-century date, and almost certainly built from the walls of the circular structure.

Ach na h-Anaite, Sarsgrum, Durness
NC 3845 6539

Another rather dubious site, this consists of a heavily-robbed mound above the shore showing quantities of small stones within its build, but much obscured by recent field-cleared stones. Once recorded as a broch, the lack of large stone and its size, put this more reasonably into the category of defended farmstead. Outwith the main enclosure on the seaward side are the remains of a ditch, now about 5 metres wide and 70cm deep. To the south, traces of an outer wall can be seen above the break of slope. Any trace of this outwork continuing on the easy, eastern approach have been destroyed by the construction of a track.

Torr a'Chorcain, Langwell, Kincardine
NC 4104 0084

The splendid setting and the good preservation of this site make it perhaps Sutherland's finest example. It is approached by a long, narrow road from Oykel Bailey Bridge along the south side of the river, or by the fishermen's bridge almost opposite the site. If the visitor chooses the latter approach, please try not to disturb any anglers, and more important still, follow the angling path upstream till you are almost under the site – the direct route across the fields means crossing electric fences around fields which usually contain several large and curious bulls. You have been warned!

The dun partly overlies an earlier, slightly unconvincing, hill-fort structure. The fort was once thought to be vitrified, but excavation found no trace of this and it is now thought unlikely. The defences enclose an area encompassing the whole of the low hill above the river, and measure about 120 metres E-W by 80 metres N-S. They mainly survive as a scarping of the lower slopes of the knoll on the north and south sides, although on the top they resemble a denuded stone wall. Here, traces of vitrified material have been reported, but they may derive from the central dun.

The dun itself is almost circular on plan, with a truly massive and heavily-vitrified wall, originally over 4 metres in thickness, but now spread to almost 9 metres in width, enclosing an area of about 11 metres in diameter. The site was excavated in part by Helen Nisbet in 1973-74, and included a section through the wall. This was revealed to be some 5 metres thick and still standing to a height of over 2 metres on its inner face. It was extremely heavily vitrified, with the core of the wall fused into a solid mass with ample evidence of the intense heat which had brought this about. Signs of molten, bubbling rock were clearly visible, as were – in places – clear signs of the empty spaces once occupied by a supporting timber structure known as 'timber-lacing'. The entrance was also excavated, revealing a 3 metre-wide gap, flanked by post holes, floored with logs, and with a guard chamber to the left of the entrance. A careful scrutiny here also reveals evidence of the timber supports (the section through the wall has now been backfilled to prevent erosion).

Within the interior a ring of large posts stood about 4.5 metres from the wall and appeared to have supported a timber and turf roof, open to the centre. Three phases of occupation were revealed, two before and one after the fire which destroyed the timber-laced walls and caused the vitrification. Radiocarbon dates range between c.440BC and 10BC with two central dates between 290-210BC. This site lies firmly within the Iron Age.

Rhaoine, Strath Fleet, Rogart
NC 6557 0512

Rhaoine is a small, almost oval dun of more conventional form. The entrance, in the south-east, leads through a wall which was probably once about 3.5 metres thick into a comparatively small space only 11.5 metres by 8.5 metres. On the inner face, some four courses survive intact on the west side, standing to about a metre in height. The site stands on a slight hillock with a steep and rocky slope on its southern side. The position commands splendid views across the valley.

Muie, Rogart
NC 6719 0457

Although rather ruinous, this is an interesting site not far above the Strath Fleet road on the north side. The inner space measures about 29 metres by 13 metres, but slopes dramatically along its longer axis. The interior therefore lies on three distinct terraces, with the entrance in the central one. The wall, much destroyed, varies from a wide spread of over 4 metres, now surviving to a height of about 70 cm, to rather thinner areas where it is now no more than 2 metres thick and only 10 cm high. A modern field wall crosses the wall at the southern end. The whole site sits on an isolated rocky hillock.

Torri Falaig, Strath Charnaig, Dornoch
NH 7288 9832

Lying within three concentric lines of defence just above the Strath Charnaig road on the south side, this much-robbed and rather indistinct site is justifiably a dun. The level interior measures 29 metres E-W by 16 metres N-S, within rather vague walls – or possibly a single wall – with a entrance, presumably, in the east where the approach is easiest. The outermost wall is probably recent, and an alleged outer trench to the south seems to be nothing more than a natural watercourse.

Wags and a Wheelhouse

Finally, there is only really one 'wheelhouse' in Sutherland, although stylistically it is more closely related to the 'wags' of Caithness and east Sutherland than the true Hebridean wheelhouses (Map 6). Like the wags, its internal divisions are formed by a series of upright stone pillars rather than the short sections of walls running inwards from the main wall to create a series of small chambers around an open, central area that are found in the Hebridean examples. Its main claim to be a wheelhouse is that is almost circular internally (Fig.12).

The wags, on the other hand (Map 6), tend towards a rectangular shape, but with rounded corners. The classic 'wag', or 'galleried dwelling', will have evidence of the supporting pillars much like those at Tigh na Fiarnain, below, but with this characteristic shape. A description of the Sutherland 'wags' (which name derives from the gaelic for "little cave") is given below, along with a small group of sites which have been described as 'homesteads' which have the *shape* of the wags without the pillars. These are most interesting sites, and desperately need further study before we can understand the relationship in space and time between all three types of site dealt with here. Don't worry about the confused terminology, just enjoy the sites!

Wheelhouse or Aisled Dwelling, Tigh na Fiarnain, Loch Eriboll, Tongue (Fig. 12)
NC 4049 6102

To reach this site, quite unique to the area, the visitor needs to undertake the long, uphill slog from the road along the west side of Loch Eriboll almost to the summit of the watershed at about 290 metres above sea level. I usually start next to the souterrain at Portnancon (NC 428 612) and follow the Allt Port Chamuill upwards, following the left stream course where it divides. This brings you to the summit plateau. Turn SW, keeping a string of small lochans to your right and cross the top of another burn. There, lurking behind a low cliff, you will find the site. If the weather is clear, you will be rewarded by stunning views eastwards towards Ben Hope and Ben Loyal across the loch.

The site's name means 'House of the Fingalians'. It stands atop a low hillock with its back to a low cliff. The main chamber is almost circular, but with one side flattened to give an overall D-shape. About 5 metres in diameter, it is enclosed by a drystone wall about 1 metre thick, and still standing 1.4m high. In the interior stand seven stone pillars which divided the area into radial compartments. One of the compartments is still lintelled, and at the time of my last visit another was partially so. Large slabs on the floor are all that remains of the rest. Whether or not the central area, within the ring of pillars, was ever roofed is a matter of conjecture, but the structure is remarkably well-preserved, and for this we should probably thank its remote location.

Looking around, it is difficult to see why anyone would have built such a complex structure in such an inhospitable position. The surrounding landscape seems entirely unfit for cultivation, and it is far from its fellows – whether they be the wheelhouses of the Western Isles, or the wags of Caithness and the eastern marches.

Outwith the main structure on the west side is an enclosure formed by setting end-set slabs into the peaty ground which has then apparently been cut out to form the enclosure. This may continue around to the north side, where a curving stretch of wall is visible. A little to the SW along the base of the rock outcrop is another vague enclosure defined by slabs set on end.

To return, retrace your steps or go round the N side of the rock outcrop and follow another burn back to the road.

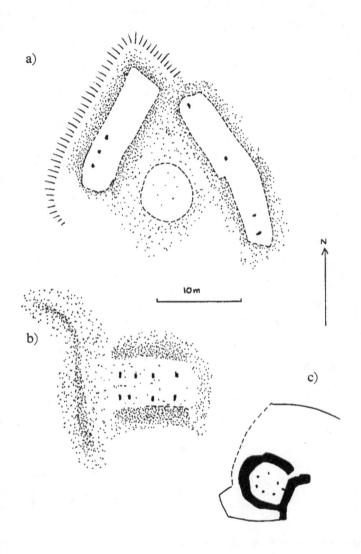

Figure 12. Plans: Wags and Wheelhouse
a) Uaigh Bheag b) Carn nan Uaigh c) Tigh na Fiarnain

Carn nan Uaigh, Glen Loth, Clyne (Fig. 12)
NC 9347 1404

Within an 19th century field enclosed by a dry-stone dyke are
the remains of two 'wags' or galleried dwellings. The name,
which means 'Cairn of the Tomb', describes what this was
once believed to be. Much disturbed and overgrown by turf,
the southerly structure is the better visible. It measures about
5 metres wide, but its original length is obscured by a later
rubble wall. The vague walls are about 2 metres thick, with
two parallel rows of upright stones – eight in all – indicating
the positions of the 'galleries'. This site much resembles the
more complete examples in Caithness. A short distance away
are the scant remains of another, only four of the vertical
supports now visible. The later, rectangular building was
reputedly built in 1798.

Uaigh Bheag, Glen Loth, Loth (Fig.12)
NC 9360 1423

Two further examples in the glen amply demonstrate the
classic 'sub-rectangular' shape. They touch at one end, and
within the rather vague pattern of their outer walls can be
seen, in one: three vertical slabs in a line towards the S end,
and in the other: 4 slabs scattered along its length and
following the slight curvature of the west side. Both are about
4 metres in internal width, with the western one 14m and the
eastern 20m in approximate length.

Druim Dearg, Glen Loth, Loth
NC 9348 1377

Yet another in the same area, this one measures 14m x 4m,
and has 4 vertical stones visible. A much later farm footing
stands adjacent and parallel to it.

Carradh nan Clach, Glen Loth, Loth
NC 9396 1256

This one lacks the upright slabs which characterise these
sites, but its general shape, and the others not far away,
suggest that this too was a 'wag'. It measures about 12m x
4m, with a semi-circular expansion at the south end.

Other sites with features which might relate them to the wheelhouse or wag structures are scattered through Sutherland in small numbers. Once referred to as complex 'hut-circles' and now as 'homesteads', their form suggests that they are more likely to belong to a post-broch period and perhaps in use during the first few centuries AD. Only excavation will clarify this in the future.

Loch Borralie, Durness
NC 3889 6702
A rather amorphous construction, with many cellular rooms within a rough oval. This seems to have more in common with the wheelhouse than the wag, as its location might suggest. The site is very difficult to understand on the ground, but the area is well worth the visit for a wide range of other sites.

Loch Brora, Clyne
NC 8526 0605
Stuck on a knoll is what appears to be a hut circle with a sub-rectangular structure attached to it. A single vertical slab close to the wall of the long building suggests a wag-like form. As the two should be of different date, this site presents a most interesting problem for excavation.

Uppat, nr Golspie
NC 8721 0182
Another example of a circular and a sub-rectangular building attached to one another. No evidence of pillars in this case.
The final list gives examples of structures which have characteristics of both hut circles and wag-like structures. None have the characteristic pillars visible.
NC 1691 4276   Slugaird Liath
Probably no more than a misshapen hut circle.
NC 7990 6266   Armadale Burn
Three compartments, both circular and sub-rectangular shapes represented.
NC 6404 0584   Bad na h-Achlaise
Again, probably an odd-shaped hut circle.

NC 7908 6327   Cromsac Hill

Three cells in a row, but its surrounding field system
suggests an odd hut circle.

NC 8569 0491   Duchary Burn

Associated with a hut circle and field system, and probably
contemporary?

NC 8331 6460   Dail a'Bhaite

Surely a multi-celled hut?

NC 9851 1813   Eldrable

This may be a hut circle with a later 'wag-like' structure
superimposed.

Crannogs

There are only some twenty recorded crannogs, or artificial
islands, in Sutherland (Map 6). This is clearly only a fraction
of what there must once have been, as crannogs are such
practical constructions. Relatively safe from attack both by
enemies and wild animals, they also occupy no useful land,
have a constant water supply and perhaps a source of food
within the water. Visibility would have been good, and
properly built they should have been as dry and warm as any
other house.

There are problems, though. Finding them can be
difficult, as any timber superstructure will long since have
rotted away, while even on small lochs, the strong Sutherland
gales can whip up waves big enough to flatten the
foundations so that they can only be seen at times of
exceptionally low water. Add to this the problem that a great
many Sutherland lochs, of all sizes, have had their water
levels raised to provide water for electricity generation, or
simply to control the flow of rivers for the highly-important
salmon fishing industry. As a result, it would only be in
exceptionally hot, dry summers – of which Sutherland has
but few – that previously unseen sites might be visible. There
could be many, many more.

Anglers or divers are most likely to find them. Those
fishing from boats are usually aware of shallow places in the
lochs where they can anchor more easily and, if investigated,
many of these might prove to be the remains of crannogs.

Any visitor who is lucky enough to be in the right place at the right time should, please, report their sighting – with a photograph if possible – to the Highland Sites and Monuments Record, whose address appears at the back of this volume. Look out for evidence of a causeway leading to the crannog from the shore. This could be the deciding feature in its identification, although not all crannogs necessarily had them.

There is one further complication here. Why did anyone *build* an island when many lochs have dozens of natural ones to choose from? I can think of no insuperable difficulty in constructing an adequate structure on an island without the effort of taking stones and dumping them in a loch to make an artificial site – yet we have no records of islands inhabited in this way. I am sure they exist but have never, I regret to say, had the time to investigate further!

As most of the crannogs cannot be visited without a boat or a swim, I merely give a list of those for which there are records. For those intrepid swimmers or divers amongst the readers – please let us know what you find!

NC 0354 3082	Loch na Claise	Crannog and causeway(?)
NC 2203 1258	Eilean an Tighe	Possible.
NC 2480 1589	Loch Awe	Possible.
NC 2480 1570	Loch Awe (B)	Possible.
NC 2574 1138	Loch Borrolan	Crannog and causeway.
NC 2636 1085	Loch Borrolan	Possible.
NC 4730 5870	Loch Hope	Crannog.
NC 5769 0685	Loch Shin	Possible. Now submerged.
NC 4730 5870	Lochside, Durness	Possible.
NC 5769 0685	Eilean a'Chairn	Two, possible.
NC 6116 4448	Eilean a'Bhuachaille	Possible.
NV 6270 5500	Loch Loyal	Crannog and causeway?
NC 6304 0710	Loch Craggie	Crannog.

NC 6313 0067	Loch Cracail Beag	Possible.
NC 6549 3821	Loch Naver	Crannog.
NC 6620 6070	Loch an Tigh-Choimhid	Island. Crannog?
NC 6780 5197	Loch nan Ealachan	Island. Crannog?
NC 7170 4016	Loch Rosail	Crannog and causeway?
NC 7396 1137	Loch Beannach	Probable.
NH 6259 9159	Loch Migdale	Crannog. Occupied 1630?
NH 6420 8800	Coill'a'Bhad-Daraich	Possible.
NH 6689 9831	Loch Bhuide	Possible. Submerged.

MISCELLANEOUS

Souterrains

The function of souterrains or 'earth houses' as they are often called is uncertain. Consisting of tunnels or chambers built below ground level and roofed over, they come in many shapes, and have been variously interpreted as refuges, shrines, animal houses, or simply stores. In Sutherland many open from within, or adjacent to, circular huts, and I would personally plump for storage every time. A chamber built below ground maintains a very steady, cool temperature whatever the weather, and these would have been ideal if kept dry. As the same principle applies to much later ice-houses, they could also have been used in this way, to store meat and fish through the winter and into the early summer. Sutherland has two main shapes – a simple passage leading to a circular or oval chamber, or a more complex cruciform type. They are most often found in association with the hut circle settlements, several actually having their entrances within the huts themselves. The distribution of known sites is shown in Map 6, although once more, there are likely to be many still to be discovered.

Portnancon, Loch Eriboll, Durness
NC 4282 6129

The visitor to this splendid, intact site should take a good torch and great care! The low, narrow entrance is marked by two stone cairns on the east side of the road – please park a few yards farther north where there is adequate space off-road. Go down a steep flight of tiny, slippery steps where you must watch very carefully where you put your feet – at the same time keeping an eye on the roof so that you don't bang your head. This is not easy! Once at the bottom, there is a short passage curving to the left, widening as it goes, to end in a roofed chamber which is still quite intact. Again be careful, as there is usually a deep pool at the bottom, and slippery mud on the floor.

The site was excavated in the early '30s by a Dr Buxton, who then laid a pipe to drain the water away. This has since failed. Little of note was found, although one suspects that modern excavation would have revealed a great deal more information. Above the souterrain is a series of hummocks which almost certainly contain the remains of a hut, but this was not investigated at the time.

Torran a'Bhuachaille, Loch Hope, Durness (Fig. 13)
NC 4689 5901

Again opening from within a hut circle, this souterrain also apparently consists of a simple curved passage with no expanded chamber. Although the roof is now collapsed, the side walling can be traced for a little way just inside the entrance. Two lintels remain *in situ*, one at its opening and another above the passage. A large earthfast boulder is perhaps another collapsed lintel. Following a curve around the hut wall reveals a depression which might represent part of the passage which has collapsed, or indeed a terminal chamber. If so, it would have been some 20m in total length.

Rosal, Strathnaver, Farr (Fig. 13)
NC 6885 4166

The abandoned crofting township of Rosal lies upon, and is intermingled with, a much earlier settlement of circular huts, and is now cared for and displayed to the public by Forest Enterprise. Take the forest road south on the east side of the river Naver from Syre junction.

Within this fascinating double complex lies the remains of a souterrain comprising a simple, almost straight, underground passage, excavated by Dr John Corcoran in 1962. The passage was unpaved, and some 13 m in length, with a sloping entrance at its SE end. Four lintels remain in place.

Kirkton, by Golspie (Fig. 13)
NH 7958 9878

From Kirkton Farm, cross the main road and go uphill through the trees adjacent to an old quarry and locate the row of cottages above the wood. A depression in the grass to the north of these, between the field wall and the wood, marks the entrance to this fine souterrain.

Kirkton is cruciform in shape, comprising two passages at right angles to one another, with expanded chambers at the ends of the two shorter arms (Plan, Figure 13). The entrance has three steps, now concealed, and a possible second entrance opens on the downhill side, now partly blocked. Again, take a torch and take care, as the floor is slippery except in the driest weather and the walls and roof have projections which can give the unwary a nasty crack. A small shale ring, now in Dunrobin Castle Museum, was found when the interior was cleared out last century. Much food refuse is reported to have lain 'on the floor', but this may be due to later reuse.

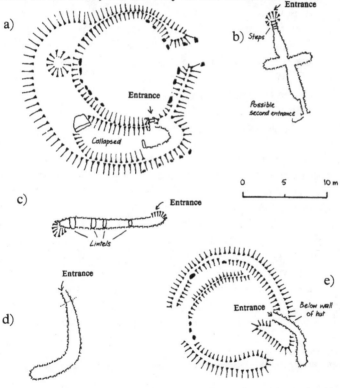

Figure 13. Plans: Souterrains
a) Torran a'Bhuachaille b) Kirkton c) Rosal d) Achinnearin
e) Caen Burn

Suisgill Bridge, Strath of Kildonan
NC 8979 2506

Presently locked to prevent sheep falling in, the site is marked by a rectangular metal cover and concrete surround outside the corner of the sheep park adjacent to the new bridge over the Suisgill Burn. The site was discovered by Gordon Barclay when investigating other features in advance of the road realignment, including a further, previously-known souterrain. The first, much reduced by earlier road-building, is protected by a metal grille at the side of the old road-line.

The new site is cruciform in shape, and much the same size as that at Kirkton. The present entry point is through the roof near the crossing, and the original entrance is not visible. The site was only partially excavated before closure.

Cos Ceumach, Kintradwell, Loth
NC 9186 0765

Not far up the gorge of the Kintradwell Burn to the west of the A9 are the remains of a souterrain excavated over 130 years ago, in 1864. It opened from the riverbank, and ran for some 10 metres into the hillside. Two expanded 'chambers' were separated by a low wall about 60cm high. Only the entrance passage is now visible for a distance of about 2 m, but depressions on the surface probably indicate the position of part of the collapsed interior. One of the stones had runic letters cut into its surface. This stone is now in the Dunrobin Castle Museum.

There is some controversy concerning the spelling of this site. The New Statistical Account calls it 'Coshgeavag', while sixty years later, in the *Transactions of the Gaelic Society of Inverness*, Volume 18, suggest it should be 'Cosh-camhaig'. The meanings of all of them seem to be 'the cave of small caves' which describes it very well!

Kilphedir Burn, Strath of Kildonan
NC 9913 1903

Another souterrain which opens from within a hut circle, this example lies amongst the splendid group of monuments which consist of the Kilphedir broch and surrounding settlement. Above the gorge of the Allt Cille Pheadair, the site opens from the best-preserved of three hut circles in the immediate vicinity. Only 70cm high and 90cm wide at its entrance, it curves to the right and downwards over some 10 m, reaching a maximum of 1.3m wide and 1.4m high at its inner end. This too is often flooded at the bottom. For a wider description of the settlement, see under *hut circles*.

Achinnearin, Suisgill Lodge, Strath of Kildonan (Fig. 13)
NC 9028 2321
Consisting simply of a curving underground passage some 12.5m long, this intact site is entered under the SE corner of a modern enclosure. Like most others, the walls are formed of boulders, with a roof of larger slabs. Ill-defined curving banks near the entrance have been described as the remains of a hut circle, but they are too vague to interpret with any degree of certainty.

Caen Burn, Strath of Kildonan (Figure 13)
ND 0106 1850
Within the widespread Caen burn settlement of hut circles (see above for a general description) is a hut with a souterrain opening from the interior. The opening lies just within a hook of thickened wall to the right of the hut circle entrance, from which a passage curves down for a distance of some eight metres. At its inner end it stands some 1.5m high and just over 1 m wide.

Other Souterrains

NC 4038 5409	**Fouhlin, Eriboll**
	Excavated. Now infilled.
NC 6655 5092	**Cracknie**
	Intact, but inaccessible.
NC 728 563	**Skelpick**
	Surface indications only.
NC 7530 8830	**Cyderhall**
	Excavated. Now destroyed.

NC 8917 2511   **Upper Suisgill**
               Mostly choked with rubble.
NC 9002 2649   **Raifin**
               Opens from hut. Collapsed.
NC 9039 2390   **Ach an Fhionnfhuaraidh**
               Ruinous.
ND 0110 1865   **Caen Burn**
               Traces adjacent to a hut.

Burnt Mounds

Burnt mounds are basically what their name suggests, and a number have already been described where they lie within settlements of hut circles. They consist of heaps of broken stone, ash and charcoal piled up in heaps either side of a central hollow most commonly seen as a cooking pit. In theory, their builders could have baked, boiled, or steamed their food with these structures.

First, make a pit in the ground, line it with stone and make it watertight with a lining of clay. Next, build a fire and heat stones upon it, then throw the stones into the pit, add food and cover. You have a simple oven. If you first put water in the pit and add the hot stones the water will boil. Add food, cover, and you have a slow cooker. Add only a little water, or add it during cooking, and you have a steamer. When finished, remove the burnt stones which are likely to have cracked with the abrupt temperature change, rake up the fire, and throw them into a heap as they are of no further use. Many burnt mounds have two heaps beside the pit – presumably where both left- and right-handed people have shovelled up the debris!

An alternative solution, or simply an alternative use, is to build a tent or wooden building around the pit, add water and hot stones, and sweat in the resulting sauna! This is quite possible, and they could have served both purposes equally well.

Burnt mounds are rarely found far from water, and most often within sight of a hut circle settlement. The distribution of recorded sites is so widespread, and so many new sites are being found with each new survey, that these are not mapped. Like crannogs, descriptions of more than 200-300 individual, known burnt mounds would contribute little to the contents of this volume, so look out for those close to sites mentioned elsewhere.

BIBLIOGRAPHY AND FURTHER READING

Close-Brooks, J., 1995. (New Edition) *Exploring Scotland's Heritage: The Highlands*, (HMSO)

Davidson, J.M., 1948. 'A Miscellany of Antiquities in Easter Ross and Sutherland', *Proceedings of the Society of Antiquaries of Scotland*, Vol.80, pp 25–33

Fairhurst, H. and Taylor, D.B., 1974. 'A Hut-Circle Settlement at Kilphedir, Sutherland', *Proceedings of the Society of Antiquaries of Scotland*, Vol.103, pp 65–99

Ford, T.D., *The Sutherland Caves*, Cave Research Group (GB), Vol.5, No.2.

Gourlay, R.B., 1984. 'A short cist beaker inhumation from Chealamy, Strathnaver, Sutherland', *Proceedings of the Society of Antiquaries of Scotland*, Vol.114, pp 567–571

Henshall, A.S., 1963. *The Chambered Tombs of Scotland*, Vol.1 (Edinburgh University Press)

Henshall, A.S., 1972. *The Chambered Tombs of Scotland*, Vol.2 (Edinburgh University Press)

Mercer, R., 1974–88. *Archaeological Field Survey in Northern Scotland* (Vols 1–3) (Edinburgh University)

Omand, D (Ed)., 1982. *The Sutherland Book* (The Northern Times Ltd)

Reid, R.W.K. *et al*, 1967. 'Prehistoric Settlement in Durness', *Proceedings of the Society of Antiquaries of Scotland*, Vol.99, pp 21–53.

RCAHMS, 1911. *Inventory of Monuments and Constructions in the County of Sutherland* (HMSO)

Ritchie, A. and G., 1988. *Scotland: archaeology and early history* (Edinburgh University Press)

Watson, W.J., 1993. *History of the Celtic Place Names of Scotland*, (Birlinn, reprint)

Wickham-Jones, C., 1993. *The Ord North, Lairg: A Journey Back in Time*, Sutherland District Council/Highland Regional Council

Those wishing to brush up on their background knowledge of Sutherland might also wish to consult:

The Statistical Account of Scotland (1790–1798)

The New Statistical Account of Scotland Vol.XV (1845) and *The Third Statistical Account of Scotland* edited by J.S. Smith (Scottish Academic Press, 1988)

Various articles by the Dr J.M. Joass, published mainly in the *Proceedings of the Society of Antiquaries of Scotland* during the last quarter of the 19th century.

The Northern Times (Golspie)

H. Morrison's *Guide to Sutherland and Caithness* (1883)

INDEX